# Are There Really Clams In Clam Chowder?

Many Ways to Raise a Family:
A Hodgepodge of Randomness

# Glenda Wilkes, PhD

Copyright © 2014 Glenda Wilkes, PhD
All rights reserved.

ISBN: 0692231218
ISBN-13: 9780692231210
Library of Congress Control Number: 2014940546
Golden Sahuaro Press,
Tucson, AZ

This book is dedicated to my husband, Jim, my life partner. Our collaboration on parenting evolved as we planned, discussed, and had fun together raising our children.

Kendall, Christopher, Adam, Amber, Courtney, and Garrett: you have provided my life's greatest learning experiences.

I am indebted to Kent Corbin for the original art shown on the cover.
To see more of his work, go to kent@kentcorbin.com.

# Contents

Introduction ................................................... ix
1—Changing Tires ............................................... 1
2—Math ......................................................... 5
3—Magic Stories ................................................ 9
4—Footie Rubs ................................................. 13
5—Clean What You Catch ........................................ 17
6—River Rocks or Things Will Never Be Equal ................... 21
7—Running Away from Home ...................................... 25
8—The Three Things that Matter Most ........................... 29
9—Logical Consequences—A Seat That Won't Tip Backward ........ 33
10—I Learned an Important Lesson .............................. 37
11—A Parent's Intuition ....................................... 41
12—Books and Reading .......................................... 45
13—Restaurant Manners ......................................... 49
14—Have a Good Day, and Help Somebody ......................... 53
15—Teacher Conferences ........................................ 57
16—No Perfect Kids ............................................ 61
17—"I Already Called Fran Swegle" ............................. 65
18—Go Places and Do Things .................................... 69
19—Addie Hooper's Mailbox ..................................... 73
20—Friends Were Always Welcome ................................ 77
21—The Animals Eat First ...................................... 81

22—Telling the Truth ............................................. 85
23—Money ............................................................ 89
24—Service to Others ........................................... 93
25—Mr. Matthews and Judging Others ..................... 97
26—The Ken-Chris Can Company ........................... 101
27—Friends as Helpers ........................................ 105
28—Use Me as an Excuse ..................................... 109
29—Never Enough Wood or Flashlights ................. 113
30—The Look on Your Face .................................. 117
31—Late-Night Free Throws ................................. 121
32—Were We a Mistake? ...................................... 125
33—Suit Yourself, Adam ....................................... 129
34—Corn Syrup .................................................... 133
35—Be Careful with Rewards ............................... 137
36—A Group of Whales Is a... .............................. 141
37—A Family Corporation .................................... 145
38—The Pit .......................................................... 149
39—Six Hundred Square Feet for Eighteen Months ........... 153
40—Captain Ate My Bite! ..................................... 157
41—Six Kids, Six Different Sports ......................... 161
42—Paul Revere and Other Nonsense ................... 165
43—Are There Really Clams in Clam Chowder? ..... 169
44—Pima County Fair .......................................... 173
45—Animal Lessons ............................................ 175
46—The Mermaid Costume .................................. 179
Addendum ........................................................... 183

# Introduction

I suppose it's a cliché to say that parenting is the hardest work you will ever do. And the most frustrating. And the most joyful. And the most rewarding. And the most disappointing. In other words, every emotion possible in the human pantry will be felt in spades in the parenting endeavor.

This book is about one family—one imperfect family. It is about the daily ideas we explored as we interacted with our children, discarding some and keeping others. It will seem much more planned than it really was. Almost everything here started spontaneously, just a spur-of-the-moment action that either produced something worthwhile or did not. The things that worked, we did again. The things that didn't work, we let go. There was much more trial and error than there was immediate success. But fortunately for all of us, children are forgiving, especially of their parents, and they have forgiven us for the things that didn't work. Or so they say.

Parenting is about paying attention. It's about being willing to engage in a daily, even moment-by-moment shared learning experience. We often think that children are the learners, learning about the world around them. And so they are. But as parents we are learners too, and nowhere does life provide deeper and more important learning experiences than in the process of helping youngsters grow to maturity. We learn about them, and in that process we also learn about us.

We may not always like what we see. For those of us who are fortunate enough to have been raised in reasonably functional families, we have good role models to follow. For those of us who may have been raised in emotionally or physically abusive families, families with alcoholism, families under continual financial distress, or any of the other ways that families can struggle, we may have come into adulthood wanting to do things differently. But how do we learn to overcome the patterns that are ingrained in our memory banks? How do we, in a moment of stress, respond differently than our parents did? How do we change those generational patterns?

It isn't easy. It takes thought, commitment, and effort every day. But when you are successful—when one day you are stressed to the max and one of your children does something so naughty that you want to respond in rage but you don't—you know something important has happened. You collect yourself and respond with the calm, rational approach you have taught yourself, and you realize for the first time that you have changed. That is a moment to put out the flag, to pour the champagne, to turn on the music and dance, and to throw confetti because you have done one of the hardest things there is to do: you have changed a lifelong pattern.

As I have mentioned, this book is about ideas. It is a hodgepodge of randomness, which is really what parenting is. Children are unpredictable. They can be difficult. They are needy. And so the response to such chaotic unpredictability is most often a hodgepodge of randomness. What I can see clearly from my vantage point now as a grandmother is that, out of that hodgepodge of randomness, we create a structure, a scaffold, a foundation upon which we build our families. It never felt organized while we were doing it. It felt so random. But today, as I look back, I can see that we were building a structure. And what I see clearly now that I couldn't possibly have seen then is that the structure is continuing in the lives of our children and grandchildren.

In this book you will meet our family, consisting of Jim, myself, and our six children: Our daughter Kendall was born first, two years later our son Chris joined us, eight years later our son Adam was born, eighteen months later our daughter Amber was born, and eighteen months later the twins, our daughter Courtney and our son Garrett made their appearance. Yes, you did the math correctly. The twins were born when Amber was 18 months old and Adam was three, so we had four children three and under, and the two older children who were 11 and 13 at that time.

At the end of the stories about our family is an Addendeum that contains several developmental theories that have direct application to parenting. I have included these few theories because I think it is important to realize that there are frameworks for helping us think about the ways in which we live our lives and in particular the ways in which we make decisions. These theoretical frameworks can help us see where we fit. We can see our actions in a larger context and perhaps learn something new. All people are life long learners. It is one of the most wonderful things about being human and participating in this wonderful adventure we call life.

There are a few questions included with each of the theories that are intended to help you apply the theory to your own experience. Additionally there are places for you to make your own notes. You will think of your own stories, your own experiences as a child, as a sibling, and as a parent. I encourage you to jot your ideas down as you read and then when you get to the Addendeum, you can go back to your notes and see how your ideas can be strengthened and enriched by the theories.

This book is intended to be fun. Have a little fun as you read and reminisce about your childhood and whatever experiences you have had with parenting children. Enjoy!

# 1: Changing Tires

It was inevitable. The call from the oldest daughter came at night, from the middle daughter in the late afternoon, and from the youngest after an early-morning soccer practice. Each had a flat tire and called her dad for help. The first time, I walked out to the truck with him and was surprised to see him put a folding chair into the bed of the pickup. When I asked him why he was taking a chair, he smiled and said, "So I can sit while I watch her change the tire."

"You mean you aren't going to change it for her?" I asked.

"No, I'm not. She is going to change it herself. I will walk her through it and tell her what to do, but my hands will be clean when we get home." And off he went.

By the time the middle daughter had her flat tire, she was able to pull into a gas station and wait for her dad to come. Again, he watched as she changed the tire under his tutelage.

The third daughter knew what to expect. She had the chair waiting when he arrived.

The interesting thing is that all three girls were **very** proud that they knew how to change a tire, had actually changed one all by themselves, and could help someone else change one if needed. It was a badge of honor.

However, much more was going on in this little scenario. What their dad taught them was self-efficacy—the knowledge that you can be successful at a given task. Self-efficacy is task specific. We can have high efficacy for math and moderate efficacy for writing, or high efficacy for soccer skills and low efficacy for playing the piano. The more tasks for which we can help our children have high self-efficacy, the higher their self-esteem is likely to be. Self-esteem is a more global estimate of how we feel about ourselves. If we are good at lots of "stuff," we are more likely to feel capable and worthwhile—the hallmarks of self-esteem.

So, as parents, we are always looking for ways to help our children be successful at tasks, such as tying their shoes, making their beds, feeding the dog, coloring, kicking a ball, being a friend, keeping their promises, and so on. These are the building blocks upon which they will navigate the often treacherous boulders of school, friendship, academic challenges, sports, and family relationships. If they feel capable, they approach the more difficult things in life with a positive outlook.

Boys often grow up with higher self-efficacy and self-esteem than girls. Why? Well, think about it. We let boys wrestle, get dirty, play hard, fight (within reason) with their siblings, talk back, interrupt, and have opinions. We tell girls to stay clean, be quiet, get along, take a back seat, be peacemakers, and take care of others. Which things do you think build self-efficacy?

At the age of 16, knowing how to change a tire and actually being able to do it was a big deal.

| | |
|---|---|
| **Activity:** | **Changing a tire** |
| **Goal:** | **Being able to change a tire by yourself if necessary** |
| **Side Benefit:** | **Bragging rights to your friends** |
| **Underlying Principle:** | **Building self-efficacy with small tasks helps build overall self-esteem** |

# 2: Math

Having grown up in the 1960s, I was not encouraged in high school to go beyond geometry, a fact I always regretted. I was good at math, enjoyed it, and realized later that I was handicapped by not having a more sophisticated understanding of mathematics. When I went back to graduate school in my forties, I went to our community college and took college algebra in order to be confident that I could be successful on the GRE and in grad school. I didn't want our children to feel they had a math deficit, and so I pushed math from the beginning with them.

When they were very young, we played math games. We had a cabin in the mountains, and from the bottom of the mountain to the top was exactly twenty-five miles. There were mileposts every mile. So, every time we went up or down, we added and subtracted and played other numbers games with the mileposts. The kids even made up their own games. We played math games with license plates, billboards, and scores from games. We let them check the addition on the bills when we went out to eat.

One evening we went out for pizza with our oldest two children who were around ten and eight years old. The waitress said there was a special that night, two medium pizzas for $16.00. We were trying to decide whether it was a better deal to get the large pizza for $14.00 or the special. We asked the ten-year-old if she would like to figure it out. We called the waitress over and asked her how big the large pizza was and how big the medium was. Our daughter took a napkin and drew two circles, one larger than the other, with the diameters of the two pizzas. Although she didn't know how to figure the area of the circles and then divide by the price to see which was a better deal, she could see by simply adding the diameters of the two mediums, comparing them to the diameter of the large, and then creating a simple ratio (although she didn't know that was what she was doing), that the two mediums were a better deal.

That daughter went on to major in chemistry and minor in physics in college; she taught high school physics in Palo Alto, California, and is now an engineer at Raytheon. Is that all because we played number games in the car and asked her to check the bills in restaurants? No, probably not. But she got comfortable with numbers early in her life, as did her sisters. Our middle daughter majored in cellular and molecular biology and writes science curriculums for online classrooms. Our youngest daughter majored in special education and teaches math to special needs high school kids. So, something "took" somewhere along the way. They became comfortable with math.

Although our three sons took different directions, they are also competent numerical thinkers. The oldest worked in the mortgage industry for years and is now in real estate investing. The other two are attorneys.

| | |
|---|---|
| **Activity:** | Playing number and math games, some of which the kids made up themselves |
| **Goal:** | Getting kids to think numerically and be comfortable with math functions |
| **Side Benefit:** | Mom and dad also learn a lot |
| **Underlying Principle:** | Being mathematically astute will help in any pursuit at any age, and self-efficacy in math, especially for girls, opens a myriad of doors |

**My Own Notes:**

# 3: Magic Stories

After dinner, the older children would settle down to homework while their dad took the four little ones to the bathtub, and I did the dishes and cleaned up the kitchen. After all were scrubbed and in their pajamas, we would read stories on the couch, and then they were off to bed with their dad.

For most of their young years, they were in three bedrooms, and their dad would rotate from room to room with the following routine. They might gather together in one room for the magic stories and then go back to their own rooms for their footie rubs, or they might just start out in their own rooms and wait for the magician to appear. In either case, there were four separate stories, one for each child. Each child would pick three things—such as a rock, a chicken, and a soccer ball—and then their dad would make up a magic story with these three objects in it. There was always wind blowing through the trees, always a good person and a bad person, and always a moral to the story. Other than that, the story could be wild and wooly, crazy and silly, or mild and snuggly.

Obviously, the kids loved these stories, and they would try and pick the most outrageous objects they could think of, assuming that there was no way their dad could make a story out of those objects each night! But, of course, he always did.

| | |
|---|---|
| **Activity:** | Telling magic bedtime stories |
| **Goal:** | Calming wired kids and getting them ready for sleep |
| **Side Benefit:** | Modeling creative thinking and the unexpected |
| **Underlying Principle:** | Time with dad, time with each other, and comfort in routine are important for a family |

# My Own Notes:

# 4: Footie Rubs

After magic stories, the next thing on the agenda each night and the last thing before the day was over was "footie rubs." As their dad went from room to room telling magic stories to the four youngest children, one of their feet in each bed would "somehow" become uncovered and, on the last round for the night, each child got a footie rub. Think how good a foot rub feels at the end of the day; it is no less calming and reassuring for a child than for an adult.

However, there was an ulterior motive. Physical touch is so important for children. It's easy to hold babies and toddlers, cuddle them, and give them ample physical affection. It's harder as children grow up to find appropriate ways to touch them, and in our culture today we are sensitive to what is appropriate and what is not. It's particularly tricky for fathers. As a mother, I had ample opportunities to hold my young children on my lap or give them back rubs, arm rubs, leg rubs, and lots and lots of hugs. And because I knew the children needed physical affection from their father as well, I encouraged him to do likewise. I knew they needed his physical touch as much as possible, so we looked for ways to "institutionalize" dad's touches. He played touching games such as "puddin' tame," a game where he grabbed a child's leg and shook it while he or she tried to grab his hand that was pretending to be a face. It was a silly game, but it was an opportunity for touching. He gave them head rubs at the dinner table and sat by them on the couch when we were watching TV. We never let an opportunity pass by for loving, appropriate touching.

The footie rub at the end of the day was his last way to say, "I love you. You are important to me. Even your footies are important to me." It was a great way for them to go to sleep at night. Daughters have a special connection to their fathers and fathers often become the "yardstick" by which girls measure all boys, and eventually all men. Providing opportunities for fathers to interact in personal and loving ways with their daughters helps girls feel secure in loving and being loved by the first man in their lives.

| | |
|---|---|
| **Activity:** | **Giving footie rubs at bedtime** |
| **Goal:** | **Helping kids relax and fall asleep** |
| **Side Benefit:** | **Being touched by someone who loves you** |
| **Underlying Principle:** | **All children, but especially daughters, need to feel secure in the love of the first man in their lives** |

# 5: Clean What You Catch

I like to think we were equal-opportunity employers when it came to our kids. They all were held to the same standards. They all worked. They all played. They all had fun. Girls cleaned chicken coops, and so did the boys. Boys did laundry, and so did the girls. Everyone got dirty, and everyone got clean.

In other words, we had the same expectations for the girls and the boys. A good example of this is our summer fishing trips to the White Mountains. We went fishing almost every summer. We all looked forward to getting out of the city and wandering up and down the fishing streams of northern Arizona. We stayed in a variety of cabins and had many adventures with wild turkeys, bear, fishing hooks, sunburns, and very tired children at the end of the day.

One rule that never changed was "you clean what you catch." This applied to all the fisher-persons. The girls baited their own hooks with slimy worms and landed their own fish. They unhooked them, put them on the stringers, and carried them from place to place. At the end of the day, they cut them open and cleaned them just as the boys did. And then they got to eat them (the fish, that is!). It was a very big deal; just ask the girls.

Occasionally the kids would bring friends along. The friends were speechless and open-mouthed as they watched the girls clean their own fish. If it was one of the girls whose friends were watching, the girls would proudly ask, "Would you like me to clean your fish for you?" And then they would proceed to actually do it. Their friends never quite looked at them the same way again.

It's a small thing in the grand scheme of things, cleaning your own fish, but there were lessons in it that were subtle yet profound. First, if you were going to take the life of something nature had produced, you needed to make good use of it. Eating fresh fish, fried in a cast-iron skillet with cornbread and beans after a long day out in the sun—could there be a better use for a trout? Second, you were responsible for your own catch. That also applied to sleeping in and then making your bed, carrying your own dishes from the table, feeding your own animals, and being responsible for your mistakes—as well as cleaning your own fish.

| | |
|---|---|
| **Activity:** | **Cleaning your own fish** |
| **Goal:** | **Being responsible for your own catches** |
| **Side Benefit:** | **Elevating yourselves in the eyes of your friends** |
| **Underlying Principle:** | **Respect for what nature offers to us** |

# 6: River Rocks or Things Will Never Be Equal

We raised our family on a five acre "city farm" with animals, an orchard, and a large garden. After twenty-two years on our little farm, we moved. We built a new home, and consequently, there was landscaping to be done. The summer after we moved in, we had a large load of river rock delivered and invited the kids to get up at five o'clock in the morning and work for two to three hours, lining a steep bank in our backyard with the rocks. Needless to say, they were "thrilled" to help out, as teenagers always are. Or not.

Our middle daughter, Amber, was working for a temp agency, so on the days that she had been called to work, she quit earlier than the others so she could get ready for work. This became quite a sore spot with the others as they drug themselves out of bed each morning to move river rock.

It has become one of those family legends that live on and get bigger and bigger with each telling. Now that they are all adults, they still remind Amber that she got off like a bandit the summer they all had to sweat and nearly die moving river rock.

It's a good example of the things will never be equal principle. I remember the spring and summer that Adam got three sets of catcher's gear for baseball. He grew out of one and one just disintegrated, so a third was purchased at no small cost. How did we justify that to the other kids? The principle.

Then there was the time that Garrett drove his dad's pickup truck into the rock pillars and damaged the bumper. For some reason that now escapes me, he didn't have to pay for the damage. Once again, the principle explains everything.

The principle is basically this: things will never be equal if you look at the short term. One child will get three pairs of shoes in one month, and another will get none. One will get to go to three movies, and the others will go to one. One will get to have two sleepovers and the others—you guessed it—none. But, if you look at the bigger picture—the long haul, the wider view, down the road—it all evens out. In a lifetime (for a child, that is twenty years), everyone gets approximately the same number of shoes, the same number of movies, the same number of sleepovers. These things are just not distributed evenly in the short term.

So when children feel sorry for themselves because a brother or sister gets to do or have something they don't, remind them that they, also, get to do and have things others don't, and that in the long run it all evens out. That is the principle.

| | |
|---|---|
| **Activity:** | **Reminding kids of the principle** |
| **Goal:** | **Helping them see that although life is not fair in the short term, it is usually fair in the long term** |
| **Side Benefit:** | **Helping smooth the waters when things don't seem fair** |
| **Underlying Principle** | **There is some logic in the world of parenting sometimes** |

**My Own Notes:**

# 7: Running Away from Home

One day the three youngest kids decided they wanted to run away from home, just to see what it would be like. Amber was nine, and the twins were seven. Since we lived in a rural area that was fairly safe, I thought it would be a good experiment. So, we packed backpacks for them with water, food, and other things they thought they might need; I kissed them good-bye; and off they went. I acted really sad, wiped tears from my eyes, and told them all the things they should know just in case they decided never to come back. They thought I was pretty silly.

As I recall, they were gone around an hour. It was summer. It was hot. They got bored really fast. They talked about walking down the road, leaving home behind them, and how that felt. By the time they were half a mile away, they wanted to come back, but they knew any self-respecting flight should last more than fifteen minutes, so they kept going. They sat down and ate some of their food and discussed what to do next. They unanimously agreed to come home.

So much for running away. This actually turned out to be an important event in their lives, more so than one would have imagined at the time. First, they were surprised that I said it was OK for them to run away. Next, they thought it would really be fun and were shocked to realize not only was it *not* fun, but also they were hardly out of the driveway before they realized they really didn't want to go. And third, they never wanted to run away again.

This was also a learning experience for me as a mother. I realized that sometimes kids *think* they want to do things that they really don't want to do, but if we balk at their requests and tell them they can't, it immediately elevates to a much higher level of desirability whatever thing it is they want to do. If it's not something that will hurt them, then it might be best to let them do it and see what happens.

I am reminded of my friend Carson, who was named after the surname of her mother's family, a very prominent family in Phoenix, Arizona. When Carson was in the third grade, she decided she wanted to change her name. The name she decided upon was Carmelita. Her mother, being wise, said simply, "Fine, go ahead," rather than bemoaning the loss of her family name, So for all of third grade, she was Carmelita Boice. Then at the end of the year, she decided she liked Carson better, and she has been Carson ever since.

| | |
|---|---|
| **Activity:** | **Running away or any number of other experiments that sound exciting** |
| **Goal:** | **Letting kids experience the disappointment of expected excitement turning into ordinariness and even boredom** |
| **Side Benefit:** | **Kids feeling in charge of their own choices** |
| **Underlying Principle:** | **Only say no when you really must** |

# 8: The Three Things that Matter Most

For us, raising children was about moving the responsibility for as many things as possible from our shoulders to theirs. Once they could feed themselves, dress themselves, make their own beds, and pick up their own toys, we no longer accepted responsibility for those tasks. And once we gave up the responsibility, we also gave up the direction they took in accomplishing those tasks. For example, from kindergarten on our children picked out their own clothes, resulting in some strange color combinations at times. Beds were not always made to our standards, but we resisted the temptation to remake them. These choices were theirs, and we stayed away from judging the outcomes as often as possible.

As they got older, we realized that the choices got more important. So, we struck a deal with them that if they would do three things for us, and do them cheerfully, we would give them as close to total control as we could over the rest of their lives. We asked them to do the following:

1. Be a part of the family and participate in family activities, work projects, clean-up projects, and family goals.
2. Do as well as they could in school. We did not expect straight A's and rarely got them, although our children were all good students. What we did expect was that they would go to class and apply themselves, do their homework, and participate fully in their education.
3. Come to church with us and participate in church youth programs consistently and without complaint.

In return for their cooperation in these three areas, we gave them control over their clothes, their rooms, their hair, their friends, their music, their extracurricular activities, and their private time. We reasoned that if the three things that mattered most to us were moving along in a generally positive direction, then the rest either didn't matter or would eventually fall into place with our expectations. And let me say here that we tried very hard to maintain a wide range of acceptable behaviors. They could step outside that range, and did at times, but because we purposely kept the range as wide as we could, they had to do something pretty drastic to get grounded or have severe consequences (more about logical consequences in Chapter 9).

| | |
|---|---|
| **Activity:** | **Agreeing to and living up to the three things that matter most** |
| **Goal:** | **Giving kids as much freedom and experience in making choices as possible while also providing a framework to make those choices** |
| **Side Benefit:** | **Kids have more freedom than most of their friends and also possibly more experience in making choices** |
| **Underlying Principle** | **Our job as parents is to little by little turn over to our children the responsibility for the running of their own lives** |

**My Own Notes:**

# 9: Logical Consequences— A Seat That Won't Tip Backward

We tried to raise our children with the Adlerian philosophy of logical consequences. In a nutshell, what this philosophy proposes is that every act has a logical consequence, and one way to teach children responsibility is to allow the logical consequence of an act to be the teacher. The beauty of this philosophy is that it removes the artificial consequence, such as a spanking, as the only consequence for all inappropriate behavior and allows something that is logical and understandable to the child to take its place. For example, if a child breaks something, the logical consequence is that he or she fixes it or replaces it. The child may have to earn the money if the item needs to be replaced, but he or she is the responsible party. If a child is not hungry for dinner and does not want to eat, that is fine. That child will go to bed hungry and will not starve by breakfast time. Time out is the logical consequence for many behaviors, such as hitting or starting an argument—if you can't be nice, then you don't get to be here—and time out is a very effective consequence because it removes the audience for the bad behavior, which is one of the strongest reinforcers of negative behavior.

The hard part to this philosophy is that sometimes you have to think quickly to come up with a logical consequence. We had a son, Chris, who loved to tip his chair backward at the dinner table. We asked him not to do this for two reasons. One, he could fall all the way backward and get hurt. Two, his younger brothers and sisters would want to try it, and their legs were not long enough to balance the chair, which would surely lead them to fall backward. Yet Chris continued to tip his chair. One night at dinner, Jim, who was frustrated, asked Chris to leave the table after three requests to quit tipping his chair. Chris demanded to know where he should eat his dinner. And Jim calmly said, "You may take your dinner to the toilet, which has a seat that won't tip backward." The other children just looked at each other with those wide eyes that said "You can't be serious. Chris is going to eat his dinner on the toilet?" Well, that's what he did, and it sort of became a legend. When company came to dinner, of course, the first child to say "You'd better not tip your chair backward or Dad will make you eat your dinner on the toilet" was rewarded with snickers and guffaws from his or her brothers and sisters and looks of astonishment from the guest.

Most of the time, the logical consequence was enough. We tried to take the term "punishment" out of our vocabulary. The only time we made an exception was for lying. If the children lied to us, they had both a logical consequence and a punishment. If they took something from someone else without asking, for example, and then refused to admit it, they had to apologize and replace it, and because they lied, they also had a punishment, such as extra chores or the loss of a privilege. Punishments were never severe or heavy handed, but they were significant enough so that it made more sense to tell the truth than not to do so.

The most important element of the philosophy of logical consequences is that it shifts the responsibility from the parent to the child. It is the child's behavior that causes the consequence, not the parent's. "I'm so sorry that **you** chose not to do your chores today, and so you'll understand that the consequence is double chores tomorrow. Perhaps you'll make a better choice from now on." It's **their** choice, not yours. And as you reinforce that over and over, they learn that they are the agents of their own destinies, that their choices matter, and that good things follow from good choices and not-so-good things follow from not-so-good choices. It doesn't take long before they get the idea and even make the same statements to each other.

| | |
|---|---|
| **Activity:** | Learning logical consequences |
| **Goal:** | Helping kids see that they make choices, and from those choices follow the consequences |
| **Side Benefit:** | They see themselves as agents who make their own choices |
| **Underlying Principle** | Each person is responsible for his or her choices |

## My Own Notes:

# 10: I Learned an Important Lesson

When our kids were in high school, they had an open campus, which means that they were allowed to leave campus for lunch. We weren't keen on the idea of them driving around town on their lunch hour, and so we had a deal with them that as long as we were paying their car insurance, they wouldn't leave campus during the day.

One day just after the lunch hour I got a call from our son, Garrett. He had been in a car accident at school. As he was leaving the parking lot during the lunch hour, another student turned right in front of him, and he hit the other car. It was not his fault. In fact, it was unavoidable on his part.

When I got to school, I saw him and could see that he was fine. When he walked over to me sheepishly, the first thing I managed to say was, "You know this wouldn't have happened if you had remembered our agreement about not leaving school during the lunch hour." Of course, he nodded his head. I went on to tell him I was sorry it happened and asked what I could do to help.

I stayed until everything was taken care of and then went home. My husband also came up to school to make sure that all the reports and everything regarding the accident were done properly. Being an attorney, that was important to him.

Later that night I was getting ready for bed, and Garrett came into my room and asked if he could talk to me. Of course, I said. He said the following: "Mom, I'm sorry about the accident. But I'm also really disappointed in something. The first thing you said to me was to remind me that I shouldn't have been leaving school. When Dad got there, the very first thing he said to me was, "Garrett, are you OK?"

I will never forget that conversation as long as I live. Letting him know that I loved him and was worried about his safety was infinitely more important that reminding he that he had done something wrong. It was an important lesson for me and one I have never forgotten.

I made a ton of mistakes as a parent. Many, many times at the end of the day I wished I had done things differently. So, I simply tried to do better the next day. I didn't beat myself up over my mistakes. I just went on and improved. Or at least I hope I did.

| | |
|---|---|
| **Activity:** | Expressing to your children that you love them and are concerned about their welfare, no matter what the circumstances |
| **Goal:** | Reinforcing that they are more important than whatever has happened and realizing that a misstep is a very important teaching moment for a parent |
| **Side Benefit:** | Creating an even stronger bond between parents and children when they realize that you still love them even though they have done something they shouldn't have |
| **Underlying Principle:** | The most important thing you give your children is the knowledge that they are loved |

# 11: A Parent's Intuition

We always tried to give our children the reasons behind what we asked them to do or not do. We did this for several reasons. First, we wanted them to see that we weren't being arbitrary and that there were in fact reasons. They might not agree with the reasons or like them, but we did have reasons. Second, we wanted to give them access to our thought processes, so they could see how we arrived at decisions, how we weighed the factors involved, and how we expressed that thought pattern out loud. We also wanted them to see that sometimes we didn't agree on the best course of action, but once the decision was made, we would back each other up and not allow them to divide and conquer.

There were also times, however, when the only reason we had was just that gut feeling, that intuition, that something was not a good idea. It was tough to get them to understand what we meant when we said, "I know you really want to go to that party, but we just don't have a good feeling about it. There is no specific reason, but we are going to ask you not to go. Let's have friends over here and do something fun here instead. We do not want you to go."

Most of the time, we got that "look" that says, "You have to be kidding me!" Sometimes they tried to mount an argument to get us to change our minds, but most of the time they knew we weren't going to change our minds. I can't think of a time when we asked them not to go somewhere and something bad happened to those who did go. But it was important for them to know that we had an intuitive sense of what was good for them to do and what was not good for them to do, and although there were times when we couldn't give a specific reason, we still asked them to trust our sense of what was right for them.

| | |
|---|---|
| **Activity:** | Asking your children to accept your intuition as a valid reason for your decision |
| **Goal:** | Teaching them to learn to rely on their own intuition and to listen to what they could learn from becoming an intuitive person |
| **Side Benefit:** | The process of explaining what intuition is, how it works, and how it could work for them too |
| **Underlying Principle:** | Parents have an intuitive sense of what is best in a given situation not only for their children but for themselves |

# 12: Books and Reading

One of the fondest memories I have of my own childhood is being read to by my father. My father was a judge and a very dignified man. He was not comfortable with frivolity or really even with lightheartedness. I was somewhat in awe of him, and being the only girl in between two brothers, I had a very special relationship with him. My favorite time of the day was after dinner and baths when he would sit on the couch and read to me. There was something about being snuggled up by his much larger body, often still in his work clothes, that was so comforting. Men just smell different than women. They smell safe and in charge and like for those few moments nothing can possibly harm you.

I think that I married my husband, Jim, because I thought he would be such a good father. After forty-seven years of marriage, I can honestly say that he has surpassed my expectations in every way and especially in that all-important category of fathering. And yes, he read to our children a lot. And so did I. We had books of every kind in our home, and one of the kids' favorites were *Zoobooks*, a monthly publication by the San Diego Zoo. Each issue was about a different animal, and the kids would read them until they were literally worn to shreds.

I have always been a reader, and that was probably what led me to wanting to be a writer. My children often saw me with my nose in a book. It rubbed off on them, as they all are readers also. But there is more to books than just the reading of them. Books can transport you somewhere else. They can ease the pain of growing up. They can lighten the load and make you laugh.

I realize that in today's world of electronic books and the myriad of electronic entertainment options that are available to all of us, especially children, the formats for reading are changing dramatically. Who knows what reading will look like ten or twenty years from now? But for my money, reading in some format that has the capacity to transport the reader to worlds of imagination, creativity, and fun is one of the best possible activities for all of us.

| | |
|---|---|
| **Activity:** | **Reading** |
| **Goal:** | **Stimulating creativity and relaxation** |
| **Side Benefit:** | **Promoting discussion** |
| **Underlying Principle:** | **Quiet time with children is essential** |

**My Own Notes:**

# 13: Restaurant Manners

We didn't go out to fancy restaurants as a family. With six children, it was too expensive. But we did go frequently to little places near home where we could eat as a family for little money. As we pulled into the parking lot and turned off the motor, we always reviewed what the expectations were. "Who remembers what restaurant manners are," one of us would ask. And then we would just very simply go over the basics: we use quiet voices; we stay at the table, and there's no running around; we're polite to each other and the people serving us; we will have to wait a little bit for our food, and we'll just talk about our day during that time.

Once everyone agreed that they remembered what restaurant manners were, we would go on in and usually everything went extremely well. Sometimes when things don't go well, it's because children don't realize what the expectations are. They don't know how long something is going to last, or they misunderstand what is expected of them. It's important to be honest with children always. If you know they're going to get shots at the doctor's office, and they ask, better to tell them the truth than have them feel betrayed. A few minutes of peace isn't worth the consequence that they won't believe you next time. It's all about expectations. The more you can help them with what your expectations are, the more they can be ready to help you. If you're going to the ballpark for a game and you have the money for everyone to have a hot dog, tell them. If you don't, tell them that also, so they know there will be no hot dogs tonight. If you're going to a movie and everyone is going to share one popcorn, tell them. If you're going shopping but only two children are getting new shoes because that's all you can afford this month and those two really need them, then explain to everyone that next month the rest will get their new shoes.

Even very small children can have good restaurant manners. Children want to please their parents. They want to make their parents happy. So, afterward, as we got back in the car, we always thanked them for having such good restaurant manner. "Yes, but so-and-so spilled her milk." Doesn't matter. "And so-and-so argued with you." Doesn't matter. Compliment all the things that went right, and forget the things that didn't, unless it was really important. If something important happened, then we might ask, "What did we learn from what happened tonight?" But that's another story.

| | |
|---|---|
| **Activity:** | **Being clear about expectations** |
| **Goal:** | **Helping children understand that expectations differ depending on the activity, location, and circumstances** |
| **Side Benefit:** | **An opportunity for praise** |
| **Underlying Principle:** | **We make assumptions that children know what we expect and then get unhappy with them when they don't act appropriately; if we are better about explaining the expectations, children often are more than willing to live up to them** |

# 14: Have a Good Day, and Help Somebody

The timing worked out that most days Jim took the kids to school on his way to work. Some days I took them, but most days he did. They would joke around in the car and sing silly songs, and just before they got out of the car, the very last thing he would say was, "Have a good day, and help somebody." They knew it was coming, and they also knew that he would ask them later about it.

Most nights we had dinner at home, together, although not always. Sometimes sports or other activities prevented a sit-down meal together. But when we did sit down at the dinner table together, Jim would go around the table and ask the kids, "So, did you help somebody today?" And then he would ask them one at a time to tell about something they did for somebody else. And then he would ask me the same thing and then relay his own experience.

The kids looked forward to this. They couldn't wait to tell what they had done. They were interested in hearing what their brothers and sisters had done. I think it fostered some ability on their part to begin to think about other people's circumstances and needs fairly early in their young lives. I think it helped them to be aware of the opportunities to be of service in small ways and to feel the satisfaction that comes when you really do help somebody else.

| | |
|---|---|
| **Activity:** | Parting words as kids get out of the car for school |
| **Goal:** | Reminding them that they can help others |
| **Side Benefit:** | Dinnertime discussion |
| **Underlying Principle:** | Everyone, no matter how small, can be of service to others |

**My Own Notes:**

# 15: Teacher Conferences

I attended teacher conferences every year, as most parents do. My children had wonderful teachers who were dedicated, skilled, and extremely patient. My children were not perfect children. Some were feisty, some belligerent on occasion, some deceitful, and some just plain ornery at times. Their teachers, to a person, helped them grow, develop, and become successful adults. From kindergarten through high school, they had extremely talented teachers, and I am grateful for every single one of them. They are the unsung heroes in the Wilkes family.

I would sit and listen while the teachers went over my children's academic progress, test scores, reading and math levels, and all the other information they had so carefully prepared for me. I appreciated their efforts to help the kids learn and progress through school. And when they were finished, I asked them the questions that were important to me. There were usually three areas I wanted to know about"

1. Do they get along with the other children? Do they share? Are they considerate of others?
2. Can they both be a leader and a follower?
3. Are they respectful of you, as their teacher, and of the other adults in the school?

Why were these important to me? First, I wanted to know how the children interacted with their peers. Were they successful at making friends? If not, then I had work to do at home. Second, I wanted to know if they could step up to a leadership role when it was appropriate, but not always be the leader. I wanted to know that they could also give others the chance to lead and themselves be good followers. And third, it was important to me that they be respectful of their teacher and acknowledge the tremendous amount of time and energy their teachers put into their work.

For the most part, the teachers were surprised with my questions. Sometimes I had to probe a little to get the answers I needed. I always made sure that I told them, "You and I are a team. Our goal is to help this child grow and develop and learn. If we can work together, we both will be more successful. I want to reinforce at home the things that you are teaching here, so please call me or send a note home whenever you see a way for me to help you with this child. Thank you for all you are doing for him or her. I am very appreciative of your efforts."

| | |
|---|---|
| **Activity:** | **Finding out about children through conferences at school** |
| **Goal:** | **Understanding a broader range of their school experience** |
| **Side Benefit:** | **An opportunity to thank their teachers** |
| **Underlying Principle:** | **Some of the most important learning that occurs in school is not about academics** |

## My Own Notes:

# 16: No Perfect Kids

I had one child who thought he had to be perfect. He was hard on himself whenever he didn't do something perfectly. This worried me. I wanted him to have permission to be less than perfect. And so, each fall, after a few weeks of the school year had passed, I would go to school and wait outside the door until the children were dismissed, and then I would ask the teacher if I could talk to him or her for a few minutes.

I would ask, "How is Adam doing? He sure loves the third grade (or whatever grade it was). Is there anything you would like me to know?" And then I would say the following: "Adam is one of those kids who thinks he has to be perfect. If he gets a 90 percent on a spelling test, the best thing you can do for him is *not* to say, 'With a little more effort, Adam, you could have gotten 100.' He is already telling himself that. The best thing you can do for Adam is to say, "You know, Adam, 90 percent is good enough.'"

Some children need a little prodding to do better. Some need no prodding, because they are always prodding themselves. As parents, we know which kids are which, and we can alter our motivational patterns accordingly. No child should think he or she has to be perfect. That is a ticket to a neurotic child. And likewise, no parent should think he or she has to be perfect, thank goodness!

| | |
|---|---|
| **Activity:** | Seeing kids as individuals |
| **Goal:** | Getting teachers to see your child as you see him or her |
| **Side Benefit:** | One more opportunity to interact with teachers |
| **Underlying Principle:** | You have knowledge and understanding of your child that will benefit his or her teacher if you can share it in a way that empowers the teacher to see your child as you see him or her |

**My Own Notes:**

# 17: "I Already Called Fran Swegle"

As parents, we often fear the worst. If a child is late getting home we imagine they are in the hospital. If we lose them momentarily in a store, we imagine they have been abducted. We want to protect them from the dangers we know are out there, and in doing so we sometimes don't give them credit for being as resourceful and self assured as they are.

The hours after school until dinnertime were particularly busy hours for our family. With all our children participating in sports and a myriad of other activities I often needed to be two or three places at once to deliver or pick up a particular child at the same time another was waiting to be picked up. They knew if I was late that I was on my way from the last pick up and they could just sit down and wait and I would be there momentarily. They learned not to panic.

If I had been in the car continuously from after school until dinnertime, as was often the case, I might not have had time to get anything ready for dinner. So, sometimes, on a particularly hectic day, we might meet at Eegee's, an Arizona restaurant chain, for dinner, coming from several different directions. On one very busy evening, we came in three cars—Jim from one ballgame with some of the kids, me from a different ballgame with some of the kids, and Kendall from a high school activity.

We had dinner and all hopped in the cars to go home. When we got home and piled out of the vehicles, someone noticed that Garrett was missing. We had left Garrett at Eegee's. I hopped back into my car and raced back to Eegee's, sure I would find Garrett weeping hysterically in the arms of some poor teenage employee.

When I pulled into the parking lot, Garrett was leaning nonchalantly against a light pole. He looked at me and cheerfully said, "Don't worry Mom, I already called Fran Swegle. She is on her way to pick me up."

Fran Swegle is a family friend who lived nearby and Garrett had memorized her phone number. Fran and I have laughed about this event over the years as she still recalls her surprise when Garrett called her!

| | |
|---|---|
| **Activity:** | **Retrieving a lost child** |
| **Goal:** | **Bringing down your blood pressure** |
| **Side Benefit:** | **Seeing your child's strengths** |
| **Underlying Principle:** | **A lot of what we think will be disastrous isn't** |

# 18: Go Places and Do Things

It doesn't cost money to take a walk around the block, go to the park, or the public library. It doesn't cost much money to go and get an ice cream cone, frequent the second-hand bookstore in your town, or take a bike ride on a second-hand bike.

The important thing is to get out of the house and see as much of the world around you as possible. Many great things are free, especially for children. Even just sitting outside in the evening and talking about the moon and the stars and how they operate in the solar system is an enjoyable experience for kids. Eating hot dogs at the local park is a big deal if you are six years old and your whole family goes and you play Frisbee or catch with someone.

The changes in the seasons and the ways the trees and flowers change are wondrous to a child. Rain and clouds, thunder and lightening provide free entertainment and terrific opportunities for learning. Trips around your city, even on public transportation, open a child's world in ways we can't imagine. Things that are ordinary to us are extraordinary to them.

We are creatures of habit. We do the same things over and over—cook the same meals, wear the same kind of clothes, go the same places. Try to get outside your habits. Go new places. Try new foods. Explore.

We went on a lot of picnics when our children were growing up. We went to local parks, we drove up into the mountains to picnic grounds. We noticed the trees and the plants and talked about what we saw and how it was different from other places. We took simple food. We took a ball or a frisbee. And we took walks around where we ate and talked about what we saw. Nothing extraordinary ever happened that I recall, but perhaps we all learned to be a little more observant of the world around us.

| | |
|---|---|
| **Activity:** | **Getting out of the house** |
| **Goal:** | **Fostering learning experiences in the world** |
| **Side Benefit:** | **Fun, fun, fun and learning to observe your surroundings** |
| **Underlying Principle:** | **There is so much to do for free or nearly free, and you can get out of your routines by simply getting out of the house** |

# 19: Addie Hooper's Mailbox

Early one Saturday morning, around 8:00 a.m., the phone rang.

"Hello, Mrs. Wilkes? This is Addie Hooper's father. I think your son and some of his friends were at my house last night."

"Really?" I asked. I knew that friends of our son's had spent the night, and they were all downstairs watching a movie until bedtime. I had taken them food several times. "What makes you think they were at your house?"

"Well, our mailbox was blown up with an explosive of some kind."

Now he really had my interest. "What makes you think it was our son?"

"Well, this morning when I went outside to survey the damage, I found Mr. Wilkes's wallet on the road beside the mailbox. I imagine they kicked it out of his truck when they got out."

I thanked Mr. Hooper for calling and assured him that the boys would be there within the hour to replace the mailbox and to apologize. Then I went downstairs to confront the culprits.

They all were, of course, still sound asleep. When I opened the door, the son in question popped his head up, wanting to know what time it was.

"It's a little after eight o'clock, and I just got a phone call from Addie Hooper's father." Three other heads popped up from various places on the floor of the bedroom. "He said that someone was at his house late last night, and his mailbox is no longer a mailbox. Do you know anything about that?"

"No, Mom, we were right here."

"Well, interestingly, Mr. Hooper says that he found Dad's wallet on the ground by the mailbox."

Long silence.

"Come on, boys, we need to go to Home Depot and get a new mailbox." And four sleepy teenagers were off to spend their own money on a replacement.

This story comes to mind for several reasons. First, Mr. Hooper called me instead of calling the police. I was very grateful for that. Second, my son's response was immediate once he knew he had been found out. Could he have volunteered the information? Yes, but he didn't. Yet when he realized we knew, he immediately knew what he had to do, which was apologize and replace the mailbox (do logical consequences come to mind?).

We talked later about a few of the horrific things that could have happened, not the least of which was injury to one or more of the boys or someone in the Hooper family. This story reminds me that there is more than a little luck involved in parenting.

| | |
|---|---|
| **Activity:** | Logical consequences in action |
| **Goal:** | Seeing if children realize what they need to do |
| **Side Benefit:** | Friends learn also |
| **Underlying Principle:** | If you give kids a chance, they will right their wrongs all by themselves |

# 20: Friends Were Always Welcome

We decided as parents that we wanted our home to be the "go to" place for our kids and their friends. That does not mean that we had a revolving door 24/7, but rather that during predictable times such as after school and before and after activities the kids were involved in with other kids, our home could be the gathering place. We wanted to create a place where all the kids felt welcome and knew that they could come to hang out without a formal invitation.

The primary draw was food. Kids will go where there is food. So, I tried always to have inexpensive food on hand to which I thought kids would gravitate. Each week I bought popcorn from a local popcorn factory in bags the size of a king-sized pillow. I also bought lots and lots of ice cream. I always had peanut butter and jelly in case someone needed an emergency sandwich before a game. We didn't drink a lot of soda pop, but there was always lemonade or something else to drink that was easy to make and could be made in bulk.

I paid close attention when a group of kids came over. I listened. I watched. Over time, I came to know the groups of friends of our children very well. I wasn't looking at manners, the way they were dressed, or other outwardly things. I was looking for the way they adapted to our home, the way they treated each other, how our own children treated their friends, whether or not they could share leadership roles and do what their friends wanted and not always what they wanted, and what they talked about. I wanted to observe my own children in the milieu of their friends and learn things about them that I could learn no other way.

| | |
|---|---|
| **Activity:** | Having friends over |
| **Goal:** | Observing your children with their friends |
| **Side Benefit:** | Learning things you wouldn't learn otherwise |
| **Underlying Principle:** | Children act uninhibited with their friends, and parents can learn a lot about them while interacting with their friends |

**My Own Notes:**

# 21: The Animals Eat First

At one time or another on our little farm, we had dogs, cats, sheep, goats, rabbits, chickens, and horses—all requiring feeding and fresh water daily. In the summer Arizona heat, if the animals went without water, the results could be disastrous. The children all had responsibility for feeding and watering the animals in the morning before school and in the evening before dinner. In the wintertime, there was ice to break up in the water buckets in the morning and cold metal lids to be removed from cans of feed. In the summertime, it was uncomfortably hot. The children also were responsible for raking pens and disposing of animal manure weekly and scrubbing out the water buckets so the water was fresh.

Most of the time, they did their chores without a lot of complaint. Sometimes they forgot. Sometimes they just didn't want to go out and do them. And therein lay the learning experiences. The rule was that the animals ate first, before the people, because they were dependent on us to feed them. Before dinner, I would remind them about their chores. And then I would *not* say anything else. When we sat down for dinner, their dad would ask them, "Are all the chores done?" It was easy to observe if they were or not. There was no use lying about it, because with six children, someone who had done his or hers would be sure to say something if someone else had not. Often just a look from one to the other would suffice to say, "Well, I did mine, but I don't think you did yours." And then because whichever children had not fulfilled their duties knew the rule, they would drag themselves out of the kitchen to go do what had to be done.

Over the years, our children really learned how to work. I have to say that all of them are very hard workers today. They take their responsibilities seriously, are successful in their chosen fields, and are teaching their own children how to work.

| | |
|---|---|
| **Activity:** | **Feeding the animals before the family eats** |
| **Goal:** | **Learning to be responsible** |
| **Side Benefit:** | **Realizing that some things just have to be done, and you might have to delay your own gratification in getting them done** |
| **Underlying Principle:** | **When you want pets and the fun of having pets, you also accept the responsibility of caring for them** |

**My Own Notes:**

# 22: Telling the Truth

No one tells the truth all the time. There are "white lies" and "whoppers" and all levels in between. I lied for years about my weight on my driver's license! We all have sensitive areas where we simply do not tell the truth. As parents, however, we want to teach our children that being truthful is not optional. In a family, we have to be able to trust that what we are hearing is as close to the truth as possible. So, we struggled with how to teach this to our children in a loving and kind way.

This is one place where example is critically important. Children are little computers when it comes to watching their parents set an example. They observe when we acknowledge receiving too much change at the grocery story or when a clerk skips an item when checking us out. They also observe when we are not honest.

One particularly harried morning, I put the kids in the car to take the oldest of the four younger children, Adam, to kindergarten. He was six at the time. His sister Amber was four and a half and the twins were three. At that time children were required to be in full-size car seats until the age of four, and then in a booster chair with restraints. We had just returned from a trip the night before with our two older children, and I had not taken the time to put all the car seats back in the car. Since I was just going down the road a few blocks, I reasoned that I could just buckle in everyone and we would be fine. We dropped Adam off at school, and on the way home, I failed to come to a complete stop at a four-way stop. Of course, I got pulled over. By that time all three of the other children had wiggled out of their seat belts and were climbing around in the back of the Suburban.

The officer looked at the three monkeys in the back seat and said very pleasantly, "How old are those two little ones?" Realizing they were supposed to be in car seats until four, I calmly said, "Oh, they're four." To which their sister, who *was* four and highly incensed that I referred to her younger siblings as being *her* age, said indignantly, "No, they're not! They're only three!"

Needless to say, I got not only a ticket for failing to stop all the way, but also two more tickets for not having the twins in car seats. And to this day, Amber remembers that I lied to the policeman.

The system that we finally arrived at for encouraging truthfulness was this. If the children did something they shouldn't do and told us the truth, there was a consequence. If they broke something, they had to replace it. If they hurt someone, they had to make amends. And so on. But, if they did something wrong and lied about it, and we found out (which we almost always did), they still had the consequence but now they also had a punishment. They lost a privilege, had extra chores, or had to give up something important to them for a while. They learned that they could get off easier if they just bit the bullet and told the truth. Did it always work? No, of course not. But telling the truth is a habit, just like anything else, and they seemed to be more in the habit of truthfulness as the years went by than hiding their misdeeds from us.

| | |
|---|---|
| **Activity:** | Creating a system for encouraging truthfulness |
| **Goal:** | Making telling the truth as painless as possible |
| **Side Benefit:** | Telling the truth becomes more of a habit than lying |
| **Underlying Principle:** | Kids make the choice to be honest or not and they reap the consequence—it isn't about you; it is about them making their own choice and being responsible for it |

# 23: Money

Money is a big deal. It is a big deal to adults, and it is a big deal to children. It's also one of those areas where children can experiment and see the logical consequences in an area that doesn't hold a lot of emotion, fear, or angst. Children learn how to use money by observing their parents and also by having some money of their own to spend. There are so many ways to do this that whole books have been written about kids and money. For us, we reasoned that as members of the family, the children were entitled to some of the family assets. Their chores were not linked to money. They did their chores because we asked them to and because they lived in a family and we all were responsible for the things that had to be done.

We gave our children an allowance weekly, in graduating amounts as they got older. It might have been $5 a week for little ones and up to $20 a week for the older ones. This was their money to spend as they wanted. They did not have to buy necessities with it, such as clothes or school supplies. They could spend it however they wanted, or they could save it up for something special.

If they wanted to spend it all on candy, they could. If they wanted to give it to the homeless guy, Rick, who lived under the bridge, they could. It was theirs, no strings attached. Because they had this kind of freedom, patterns emerged quickly, and it was often interesting to talk about the consequences of these patterns. We tried not to be judgmental about how they spent their money. Our role was to help them see what happened as a result of the choices they made. I don't remember now how any one child spend his or her money. I guess I just didn't pay attention because it was their own deal. And if I told them it was up to them, then I truly did try to take myself out of the decision making process.

Most of all, we didn't want money to be tied to love. We didn't want it tied to acceptance. We didn't want it tied to their feelings of importance. It was just money.

| | |
|---|---|
| **Activity:** | Giving an allowance |
| **Goal:** | Giving kids the opportunity to experiment with money |
| **Side Benefit:** | When the choices are theirs entirely, patterns emerge, and sometimes you can help them see things they can't see themselves |
| **Underlying Principle:** | Money is just money |

# My Own Notes:

# 24: Service to Others

Jim and I were very aware that we were living and raising our family in very favorable circumstances. We had everything we needed and most of what we wanted. We did not consider ourselves wealthy, but by the standards of the world, we certainly were. We were appreciative every day of the things people often take for granted—good health, a home, freedom to make our own choices, jobs, friends, and many more elements of our lives that blessed us as a family.

I had been raised in a home where my parents were always helping others. My father started the free lunch program for children in our city and worked tirelessly on boards such as the Square and Compass Crippled Children's Clinic and others. My mother, as a stay-at-home mom, was continually volunteering in church programs and other less visible ways of helping those in need. It was just a way of life. And it was a way of life we wanted our children to experience.

We participated as a family in several organized efforts such as adopting a needy family at Christmas and letting the children participate in purchasing and wrapping presents, preparing a meal, and then delivering it all. We went to the Community Center early Christmas morning for many years and helped prepare the meal for hundreds of individuals. We usually prepared all the mashed potatoes. After the food was prepared, we manned the warmers, delivering large metal bins of food to the servers who prepared the plates for those who came. After the noon meal was over, we helped make boxed lunches for people to take home with them or for drivers to take to shut-ins. We arrived at 8:00 a.m. and stayed until after 4:00 p.m. We all went home exhausted, but what a wonderful way to spend Christmas Day as a family.

These efforts were important because we could do them as a family. But more important was the underlying element of watchfulness, eagerness to be of assistance, and nonjudgmental intervention when necessary that we tried to teach, emulate, and foster in our family. There are a hundred small things we can do for others that are never noticed by anyone but that person. It is those small acts of kindness that we offer to others for no reason other than that we see what they need and are in a position to do it. So we do. And we don't ask for any recognition because of it. If we have left our children with anything, we hope it is the desire to serve others.

| | |
|---|---|
| **Activity:** | Providing opportunities to be of service as a family |
| **Goal:** | Being of service to others as a way of life |
| **Side Benefit:** | Too many to mention |
| **Underlying Principle:** | We have so few ways we can be truly grateful for our blessings, and being of service is the best way to do this |

**My Own Notes:**

# 25: Mr. Matthews and Judging Others

Our little farm of five acres had originally been part of a much larger piece of land owned by William R. Matthews, Jr. He still lived on a large, fenced property north of us adjacent to a large wash that had water in it from summer rains as well as winter snow melts on the Catalina Mountains. When we first moved in, wanting to be neighborly and also wanting to meet Mr. Matthews, I made cookies and walked back to his house. I had to go through a very large, black wrought iron gate, and I noticed, somewhat belatedly, that there were black skulls on the tops of the wrought iron posts that made up the gate. You could not see his house from our road, and I had never been back there. It was overgrown with large mesquite trees, and as I walked down his dirt pathway to his house, I wondered if it was a good idea. I knocked on the door and after a wait, he opened it and said gruffly, "Who are you?"

I explained that we had just moved into a guesthouse on the property in front of him and would be building a home there for our family, and I wanted to introduce myself. I swear I am not making up what happened next.

He looked me straight in the eye and said, "I live back here because I want to be left alone. I don't like people, and I don't want you to ever come here again. And if your children ever come onto my property, I will not hesitate to shoot them." And he closed the door, after he took the cookies.

I walked back to the little guesthouse the four of us were living in and sat down on the porch to collect myself. That night, Jim and I talked to the kids, who were then eight and six. We explained that Mr. Matthews wanted to be left alone and that we should not go across his property line for any reason, even to retrieve something that was ours, such as an errant ball or a dog or anything else. We should always be polite to Mr. Matthews if we saw him on the road or walking down to get his mail, but we should never go to his home for any reason.

Years passed, and we frequently saw Mr. Matthews on the road. We even stopped and visited with him if he was walking. He often took a taxi to the grocery store, and sometimes when we saw him, it was obvious that he had been drinking. We were always friendly, but the kids were a bit afraid of him, which was probably a good thing.

One day I was at a board meeting for the Casa de los Niños Crisis Nursery, and another one of the board members asked me where I lived. When I told her, she asked if I lived near Bill Matthews. When I told her yes, he lived right behind us, she asked me how he was. I relayed the story to her of the cookies, and she said sadly, "I grew up next door to him. His father used to lock him in the shed outside when he misbehaved and leave him there all night. I wondered what would become of him."

That night, at home, we talked for a long time with the kids about Mr. Matthews. We talked about all the ways we had judged him, and we talked about how unfair we had been in our judgments, knowing now the terrible abuse he had endured from his father. We talked as a family about judging others—how easy it is—and how wrong we usually are in those judgments. We learned a powerful lesson from Mr. Matthews, one none of us will ever forget.

| | |
|---|---|
| Activity: | Family discussions about judging others |
| Goal: | Making the implicit explicit; actually talking about our underlying value and belief systems and when they might not be accurate |
| Side Benefit: | Giving all members of a family a chance to voice their understanding |
| Underlying Principle: | The way we act is based on the way we think, and the way we think is to some degree based on our underlying values |

# My Own Notes:

# 26: The Ken-Chris Can Company

When Kendall and Christopher were around twelve and ten, they asked us if we would buy them an Atari. It was the newest thing for kids their age and the first of the electronic games. It was all very exciting for them, and they really, really wanted one. The game systems were around $100, as I recall, and that was more money than we thought we should spend on a "toy" for them, and their allowance wouldn't be enough to supply them with one before they left for college. So, we explored what the options were. We finally decided on a plan. We would open a savings account at the nearby bank and name it the Ken-Chris Can Company. Every Saturday, one of us would take them to the nearby parks to collect aluminum cans from the garbage bins to take them to the recycling center. If they were diligent, they could save up enough money for the Atari in three months.

They kept their part of the bargain, and I still have the passbook for the Ken-Chris Can Company. They accumulated enough money, purchased the Atari, and life was good. But much more importantly, they saw that they could set a goal, even a very long-term goal (three months was an eternity to them at the time), and with effort they could reach it. And think of all the fun they had along the way digging those aluminum cans out of the trash bins at the park!

| | |
|---|---|
| **Activity:** | Working for and saving funds earned for a purchase |
| **Goal:** | Delaying gratification; teaching appreciation for the ability to acquire the things we want and need |
| **Side Benefit:** | Setting up an accounting system with a timeline of how long it will actually take to earn enough money to purchase the item |
| **Underlying Principle:** | We all appreciate more the things for which we have to work |

# 27: Friends as Helpers

There is always work to be done on a farm, even on a city farm, and since there seemed to be a never-ending supply of kids at our house, frequently we enlisted the aid of our children's friends to accomplish tasks that needed to be done. Moving a woodpile, clearing an area of rocks so we could lay sod for a playground, weeding the garden, building an animal pen, or taking bales of hay out of the truck and stacking them in the barn all qualified for using friends as helpers. The kids used to complain loudly that their friends were going to quit coming over if we didn't stop using them as laborers. But, funny thing, they never did. In fact, they seemed to enjoy helping. They enjoyed it a lot more than our own kids did.

Girls and boys helped alike—we were equal opportunity employers. At our house, the chores rotated among the kids irrespective of gender. Boys did laundry, dishes, and cleaned bathrooms. Girls cleaned horse corrals, built animal pens, and birthed baby goats. In fact, one of Courtney's favorite chores was going out on the grass after her dad came home from work and gathering up the dead rabbits he shot with his .22. I really hate to admit this in writing, but we were a bloodthirsty group who considered the height of amusement the chopping off of the heads of the old chickens who were no longer laying and watching the bodies flutter around until they died. I do not recall that we asked their friends to participate in such activities, but our kids seemed to enjoy them. I actually objected, but to no avail. I hope there are no lasting abnormalities from such wanton savagery, but you'd have to ask the kids.

But the point is that we enlisted the help of our kids' friends if they were around and something needed to be done. They seemed to understand it was just the price of admission to the Wilkeses' farm, and I have to think in looking back that because they enjoyed being at our house, they were more than willing to lend a hand when asked.

| | |
|---|---|
| **Activity:** | Asking kids' friends to help with routine chores |
| **Goal:** | Getting kids to realize that chores don't go away just because friends spent the night |
| **Side Benefit:** | Counterintuitively this elevates kids in the eyes of their friends—they have significant responsibility and are expected to fulfill their obligations |
| **Underlying Principle:** | If you can't be happy working, you'll never be happy because most of life seems to revolve around one form or another of work |

# 28: Use Me as an Excuse

We had kids spend the night at our house a lot. We had room, and it was not unusual for us to fix breakfast in the morning for our six and an equal number of sleepover friends. Likewise, our kids frequently spent the night at their friends' homes. We were well acquainted with the parents of these friends and never felt uneasy about them spending the night. We did offer them an out, however, if at any time the kids felt they wanted to come home. We told them to use us as an excuse. If something was going on that they felt uneasy about, they could simply say, "I wasn't feeling very well earlier today, and my mom said if I got here and didn't feel well to call her and she would come and get me. She wouldn't want me to give whatever I have to you. I think I should call my mom and have her come get me because I'm not feeling well."

It didn't happen often, but each of the kids at one time or another called us to come and get them. The reasons varied, and they didn't matter. What mattered was that they had an out, and they could save face and come home. And they did.

| | |
|---|---|
| **Activity:** | Calling parents to come and pick up kids |
| **Goal:** | Teaching kids that they never have to stay in an environment that makes them uncomfortable for any reason |
| **Side Benefit:** | Giving kids control over themselves |
| **Underlying Principle:** | There are always options; you are never stuck. You may feel stuck, but you really aren't. You can always find a way to get out of a bad place if you put your mind to it |

# 29: Never Enough Wood or Flashlights

We all have our fetishes—things we love, things we have too many of but still want more. For some, it is kitchen gadgets, collections of books, quilts, vintage cars, or art. We just love what we love. For Jim, it was wood. He was attracted to cords of wood like a cat to a ball of string. One of his favorite sayings was, "there is never enough wood." He would stop at a roadside wood seller and bargain his way into the best cord of wood. The back of our property must have contained forty cords of wood, all stacked neatly, row by row, but if there was another cord to be added, he wouldn't hesitate to do so.

Second only to his love of wood was his love of flashlights. He had every size, color, and kind of flashlight, and once again the mantra was "you can never have too many flashlights." One could speculate all the psychological reasons for wanting to collect wood and flashlights, but that would be far above our purposes here. The important thing about wood and flashlights was just accepting them as Dad's quirks. Mom had her quirks too. And guess what? Each of the kids had his or her quirks.

One of the wonderful things about families is that we get to play out our quirks in the safety net of people who love us and accept us, quirks and all. Most quirks are harmless. Some can be irritating. But we all have them, and we need to learn how to accept them in others. To this day, the kids tease Jim about his woodpile, and guess how many flashlights we have at the cabin? Way too many.

| | |
|---|---|
| **Activity:** | Laughing at our quirks |
| **Goal:** | Realizing we all have quirks, most of them harmless |
| **Side Benefit:** | Learning to be accepting of one another and of all people |
| **Underlying Principle:** | We are all different, and whereas individually we may seem strange, collectively we bring strengths to our family, and even our quirks can be fun and entertaining |

# 30: The Look on Your Face

When Adam was about six or seven, I asked him to pair up the socks on the counter top in the laundry room after I had done the laundry one day. He trudged in there and was out in a respectable amount of time. But something was fishy. I asked him if he had paired up *all* the socks, and he said yes, with the most innocent look on his face. Way too innocent. I was sure he hadn't. I walked into the laundry room and he had very carefully paired up three or four pairs and laid them lengthwise across the rest of the pile of unmatched socks. Busted! I went and got him and asked him to please finish the job. He asked me how I knew he hadn't done it the first time. I told him, "By the look on your face."

When you have children, you begin a life of intense observation. You watch those children day after day. You watch them smile, roll over, crawl, learn to feed themselves, take baths, play, and all the other things children do that delight and amaze you. And you learn, if you are paying attention, what the slightest changes in their facial expressions are telling you. They don't have to say one word. You know. And that is why you can tell when they are telling the truth and when they are not. It always amazed our kids that we knew most of the time whether they were being truthful with us long before they confessed. We knew by the looks on their faces.

| | |
|---|---|
| **Activity:** | Watching the looks on your children's faces and learning the nuances of what those looks tell you |
| **Goal:** | Becoming so familiar with your children that you can tell by looking what they are thinking |
| **Side Benefit:** | Just one more avenue of insight into your children |
| **Underlying Principle:** | As a parent you know your children better than anyone, even better than they know themselves. You can use that knowledge to help them learn about themselves. When they know themselves as well as you know them, your real work is done! |

# 31: Late-Night Free Throws

We had a basketball court in our backyard, and it was not unusual for the boys and their dad to be out on the basketball court playing a game of "Horse" or "Pig" into the wee hours. Many nights, way past midnight, they were out there. I stayed away, partly because I didn't want to interrupt the conversations that were taking place, and partly because it was just the boys. And partly because I was probably headed to bed.

It was never too late to start a game, and they just kept going until they were finished. To this day I do not know what they discussed. Mostly sports, I imagine. But I also imagine there was a fair amount of teaching going on out there that had nothing to do with sports or school.

It was sort of their private territory and their private time. And in looking back, I suspect it was one of the very important things that happened between these boys and their father. It wasn't a campout where there were lots of fathers and sons. It wasn't a baseball field or a soccer field where there was a team of boys. It was just a boy, brothers, or brothers and their friends and one dad.

I do recall that most of the time, their dad won. In fact, most of the time, he skunked them. It's kind of like the ice cream tally they now have when they play golf. I think they owe their dad in the hundreds of ice creams because he gets them so distracted when they play that they can't make a putt for the life of them. I think it all started on the basketball court late at night when he distracted them with silly jokes and they couldn't make a free throw if their driver's licenses depended on it.

Whatever happened out there, I know it was meaningful to all of them.

| | |
|---|---|
| **Activity:** | Late-night hoops |
| **Goal:** | Simply spending time together |
| **Side Benefit:** | A perfect time to talk about deeper things |
| **Underlying Principle:** | An ordinary activity, done over and over, can provide a platform for heavy talk |

# 32: Were We a Mistake?

Our youngest children are fraternal twins, a boy and a girl, and they were born eighteen months after their next-older sister. Although we might have had more children anyway, we were not planning on more that soon. It turned out to be a wonderful blessing, and we are so glad they came when they did. All along I was honest with the other adults in our family about the unexpected nature of the pregnancy.

One day, Courtney, one of the twins, who was probably six or seven, came up to me in the kitchen and very quietly asked, "Mommy, were we a mistake?"

Obviously she had heard someone say something, and she needed to know. I was in a bind. I didn't want to lie to her, but I also wanted her to know how much I loved her. I thought for a minute and this is what I said:

"Courtney, there is a difference between a mistake and a surprise. A mistake is something you wouldn't do over again, and a surprise is something you would. You and Garrett were a wonderful surprise."

She stood there for a minute, pensive, but then looked up at me, smiled, and skipped out of the kitchen.

"Whew," I thought to myself. For once I think I said the right thing. The important thing was that I had told the truth. She would have known if I had lied, and that would have damaged my relationship with her. Most of the time we can tell the truth and still be careful with someone else's feelings, especially children. It's also OK to say, "Let me think about that for a minute. Can we talk about it in five minutes?" If you are unsure what to say, you can buy some time and perhaps come up with an answer that is both kind and truthful.

| | |
|---|---|
| **Activity:** | **Answering your children's questions** |
| **Goal:** | **Always being honest with them** |
| **Side Benefit:** | **They learn to trust you and will come to you with their questions, giving you—not their friends or the Internet—the opportunity to teach them important things first** |
| **Underlying Principle:** | **Honesty is always the best policy, and children will feel betrayed if they find out you have been false with them, damaging your credibility** |

# My Own Notes:

# 33: Suit Yourself, Adam

Adam was probably around six when he came stomping up the stairs from the basement one day, crying loudly.

"Mom, Kendall called me a swear word," he sobbed.

"She did? What did she call you?" I asked incredulously.

"She said, 'Suit yourself, Adam!' And I know that's a swear word!"

Obviously Kendall was angry at Adam for something, and the tone of her voice carried a stronger message than the words themselves. Adam was sure he was going to get her into trouble by telling me she was swearing at him.

So many times in families, children aren't listening to what you are saying, but they are internalizing—to a profound degree—the *way* you are saying it. Your body language, your tone of voice, and everything else about your demeanor is continually giving them messages about whether they are valued and loved.

You can say something very hard for someone else to hear, but if you say it kindly and at the same time reassure that person that he or she is important to you, that person will hear your message differently. Or you can say something very neutral but say it in a very angry voice, and the emotion overpowers the message itself.

| | |
|---|---|
| **Activity:** | Expressing disappointment and even anger in a way that does not demean or frighten your child |
| **Goal:** | Being authentic in what you say because we all get angry and we all get disappointed, but we need to do so in a way that shows control of our emotions and never causes a child to be afraid of what will happen next |
| **Side Benefit:** | Modeling for children that adults can exercise self-control even when they are angry, and by implication the expectation that they can too |
| **Underlying Principle:** | Children are intuitive, and they are very smart. They know what emotion is being conveyed regardless of the words we use. So if our words and our emotion are in sync, we create a safe world for children where they can anticipate respectful treatment no matter what the situation |

# 34: Corn Syrup

Our youngest son, Garett, was chronically ill as a young child. He was hospitalized with respiratory syncytial virus when he was seven weeks old and was in ICU for ten days. They gave him a fifty-fifty chance of survival. Even after that, he seemed to catch every virus that came along, had chronic ear infections, and seemed to always be sick.

He was also a difficult child behaviorally. He had temper tantrums, was speech delayed, and in general was difficult to manage. We loved him, and we gave him a wide berth at home, but often in public we were aware that his behavior was problematic.

One Sunday at church when he was in the hallway being asked by his Sunday school teacher if he could please behave, one of the other mothers said to me, "You know, Garrett reminds me a lot of my son at that age. Someone suggested to me that he might have a food allergy, and sure enough we found out he was allergic to corn. We took him off all corn products, and the difference was amazing. You might want to try it with Garrett."

Well, she had my attention. I asked her to explain how I would do that, and we gave it a shot.

Basically for one month we took him off the five major food allergens: sugar, corn, wheat, milk, and chocolate. And we saw his behavior improve dramatically. Then we reintroduced them one at a time. Milk came first—no problem. Wheat came next—no problem. Corn came next—and bingo! With fifteen minutes of having corn flakes for breakfast, he was having a tantrum.

We took our entire family off all corn products for the next five years. I read every label on every product I purchased and came to know all the code words for corn—dextrin, malto dextrin, and the most insidious of all, corn syrup, which is in just about everything. We ate mostly a natural diet.

I would have not believed the difference if I hadn't seen it with my own eyes. Garrett was a completely different child. He was happier and manageable, made much better choices, was sick less, and improved in school. It was amazing.

Since then I have often wondered how much of hyperactivity is due to diet. I had no idea how much corn products we were eating every day in bread, cereal, crackers, canned products, and even frozen products. When we eliminated them, we eliminated much of the source of his problem.

You might be interested to know that Garrett has been a wonderfully successful adult. He is kind, generous, loving, quick-witted, athletic, and very fun. He is a practicing attorney, is married to a wonderful woman, and has two adorable children. So, the pot of gold was definitely at the end of the rainbow.

| | |
|---|---|
| **Activity:** | **Eliminating an allergen from the family's diet** |
| **Goal:** | **Modifying behavior through natural methods** |
| **Side Benefit:** | **Demonstrating to children that you are all in this together, and if not eating or doing a certain thing helps a family member, it is a small price to pay for his or her wellness** |
| **Underlying Principle:** | **It is a privilege to make sacrifices for one family member, and it draws us closer as a family** |

# 35: Be Careful with Rewards

When Adam was ten or so, we took him to a university football game with us. He was having a wonderful time and at halftime asked if he could walk down to the concession stand by himself and get a soda. His dad said sure and gave him $20 since that was the smallest bill (and probably the only one) he had in his wallet. Adam seemed to be gone for a very long time, and when he came back, his dad asked him for the change. He said he didn't have any, as he produced a bag with several other items—a bobble-head doll, a pennant, and so on—that he had purchased with the $20. We laughed. Our mistake, obviously. Who would give a ten-year-old $20 and expect him to buy a $2 soda and that is all? Us, apparently.

What does this have to do with rewards? In our culture, we are very hung up on self-esteem and want our children to have high self-esteem. Consequently we verbally reward them for everything they say and do. And as they get older, we give them material rewards that are often greater than the accomplishment being rewarded would warrant.

In our family, we were careful with rewards. We never rewarded with money. In high school our kids would lament that their friends' parents paid for good grades. Not us. The feeling of accomplishment was their reward. Our kids drove old pickup trucks to school, wore clothes until they were worn out or too small, had inexpensive furniture in their rooms, and so on.

The one consistent verbal reward we gave them often was telling them that they were smart and could figure things out for themselves. From the time they were little, we gave them things to solve and then delighted with them in the realization that the solution had come from their very-own smart minds.

Back to the football game—$20 was an inappropriate amount of money for a soda. We often, in our desire to give our children high self-esteem, give them $20 when $2 would be just fine.

| | |
|---|---|
| **Activity:** | **Verbal and material reward giving in a family** |
| **Goal:** | **Making the reward appropriate to the action** |
| **Side Benefit:** | **Kids learn to rely on their own capability and not on external rewards for their feelings of self-worth** |
| **Underlying Principle:** | **The feeling of accomplishment that comes from working at something and doing it well is the greatest reward we can experience, and we rob our children of feeling that by thinking we have to give them something every time they do something well** |

# 36: A Group of Whales Is a...

There are so many ways to teach children about the world around them that the options for fun and creativity are endless. One thing Jim did with our kids was play games about animals. His knowledge of flora and fauna was extensive, and he would quiz the kids at every opportunity about what they were seeing and experiencing in the world around them.

One of their favorite games was knowing the various names for groups of animals and their young. For example, a mother whale is a cow; a father whale is a bull; a baby whale is a calf; and a group of whales is a pod. A mother turkey is a hen; a father turkey is a tom; a baby turkey is a poult; and a group of turkeys is a rafter. The list of animals and their categories is seemingly never-ending—trust me—trips to San Diego *and* back have not exhausted the supply. And some of the names are so interesting and unusual that they provide for much laughter and astonishment.

I'll never forget the day Courtney came home from school and said her teacher wanted to know what a female donkey was called and that she was the only person in the class who knew it was a jenny. She felt very accomplished in her knowledge of jacks and jennys. Thank you very much, Dad.

| | |
|---|---|
| **Activity:** | Word games |
| **Goal:** | Fostering an appreciation for the variety of the world around us |
| **Side Benefit:** | Learning trivia that may or may not come in handy later |
| **Underlying Principle:** | You can engage kids in simple things that are lighthearted and fun. Every adult has this kind of knowledge, be it tools, cars, songs, trees, flowers, weather, clouds, rocks, or minerals. The list is endless, and kids love to be engaged in these kinds of mind games |

# 37: A Family Corporation

I'm not sure exactly why we did this, but at one point we created a family corporation, with a document similar to a constitution, a flag, and a motto. It seemed like a good idea, and in retrospect, I think it was. It made the kids feel a part of something special—something that was bigger than just each of them individually.

Along with this we held family council meetings once a month. It was a time for anyone to discuss anything that was on his or her mind. No topic was off limits, and everyone had to respect everyone else's opinion. We planned family trips, changed chores, discussed anything that was bothering anyone, thanked individuals who had helped out or gone out of his or her way to do something nice for another family member, and so on. Sometimes the meetings lasted ten minutes, and sometimes they lasted an hour.

Kids could request an increase in their allowances or later curfews. Parents could request a change in behavior of some kind. And kids could make requests of one another without a parent intervening. It was a good practice ground for the kids trying to work through an issue with us in the background in case they needed us, but for the most part we stayed out of it and let them resolve it.

We tried to formalize the structure of our family to make it real to the children. We wanted them to know that they were a part of something bigger than themselves, and they were important and integral to its well-being. Sometimes we engaged them in decision making about whether to go on a family vacation or buy something they wanted for the house. Their opinions mattered, and we listened to what they had to say.

| | |
|---|---|
| **Activity:** | Formalizing a family structure without making it stuffy or overbearing |
| **Goal:** | Providing a structure and a feeling of belonging |
| **Side Benefit:** | Kids feel like their opinions really matter, and they do |
| **Underlying Principle:** | If kids see how decisions are arrived at, especially where money, time, and resources are involved, then they will be more able to employ those methods in making their own decisions |

# 38: The Pit

A landmark in Tucson, Arizona, was the Pioneer Hotel. For decades it was the nicest hotel in Tucson, and when it was severely damaged in a fire in 1970, it was a devastating event for the whole community. In the 1980s the hotel underwent a major renovation, and as part of it the old boiler room was closed down for a more modern heating system. The old firebrick that had lined the boiler was going to be discarded. And so Jim took Kendall and Christopher, who were around ten and twelve years old, down to the hotel, and they crawled into the boiler room and carried out the firebricks one by one until they had a pickup truckload of firebrick from the Pioneer Hotel.

They brought the bricks to our little farm where we dug a barbecue pit and lined it with these firebricks. It was our first pit of what has since become a family tradition of deep-pit barbecuing. We have dug a pit at the two homes we have had since the farm, and each year at Thanksgiving we invite friends and neighbors to cook a turkey in it. It has become quite a production over the years, and we now put forty-five to fifty turkeys, pork loins, and other items in the pit each fall.

This event comes to mind for several reasons. The use of the Pioneer Hotel firebrick was important to us because of the heritage of the old hotel. We like paying attention to the heritage of our community. Secondly, the pit is something we all do together every year as a family. Even today, with all six children married with children of their own, they all gather at our house for the pit. And lastly, it preserves our own family tradition of serving others. It is a way we can say thank you to people outside our family for their care and concern for us. Everyone participates. Amber makes all the sacks for the turkeys. The boys monitor the fire all day until the coals are just right. I check the turkeys in all day as they are delivered by friends. Jim gets the spices ready. The boys set up the work tables around the pit for washing, seasoning, and wrapping all the turkeys. Around four in the afternoon on Wednesday, the family springs into action, and in two hours all the turkeys are made ready to lower into the pit through an elaborate family assembly line. Around six the pit is covered, and the meat cooks all night. At ten in the morning, everyone comes to get their turkeys, which are marked with a metal tag with a number, and Kendall is the keeper of the master list of whose turkey is whose. The taster comes out first—a turkey and a pork loin—and is opened for everyone to taste. Then the rest come out and are matched with their owners.

Then our family stays by the pit after everyone is gone and shreds and packages our meat for the freezer. This may take several hours, and then we have all the clean up to do. And then we have our own Thanksgiving dinner.

| | |
|---|---|
| **Activity:** | **Cooking turkeys in a pit** |
| **Goal:** | **Preserving a family tradition of service to others** |
| **Side Benefit:** | **Having a lot of fun together as a family** |
| **Underlying Principle:** | **It's important for there to be activities in a family that become traditions. Each family comes upon these in a unique way. It gives comfort and safety to children to know that at certain times of the year, certain traditional activities will happen** |

**My Own Notes:**

# 39: Six Hundred Square Feet for Eighteen Months

When we bought our five acres of land and decided to build a farm for our family, we first built a small guesthouse that was twenty by thirty feet. It had one bedroom, one bathroom, and a small kitchen and living area. Jim, Kendall, Christopher, and I moved into this little house while we built the main house adjacent to it. We expected to be in the guesthouse for six months. Since we were the contractors for the main house, and since we had no idea what we were doing, the construction of the main house took much longer than anticipated. We ended up living in the guesthouse for eighteen months.

Most of our things were in storage. We had taken only what we had to have to the guesthouse. When moving day came and we brought all the boxes from storage to the main house, we were surprised at how many there were. And as we started unpacking them, we realized that we had existed perfectly well without most of the things that had been in storage for eighteen months.

In fact, we had gotten along quite well in six hundred square feet of living space and with only a small amount of clothing, dishes, and furniture. At some point we wondered if we really needed the main house after all and certainly whether or not we needed all the "stuff" we had been storing.

If we could pare our lives back to what is really essential, I wonder what amount of "stuff" that would be. We lived a pretty simple life for those eighteen months. We built a garden. We built animal pens. We got chickens and goats and bees. We grew a lot of what we ate. We didn't need a big house to do any of those things.

| | |
|---|---|
| **Activity:** | **Living smaller than you think you can** |
| **Goal:** | **Paring back to what is really necessary** |
| **Side Benefit:** | **Realizing that "stuff" isn't necessary** |
| **Underlying Principle:** | **The importance of keeping "stuff" in perspective and remembering it's really just "stuff"** |

# 40: Captain Ate My Bite!

Most of the spontaneous games that were created in our family came from Jim. He was the one with the lightheartedness and silly sense of humor, which the kids loved, and, of course, that encouraged him to be even sillier. Only one or two of these spontaneous games that have survived came from me.

My mother grew up in the Depression, and she often went to bed hungry. So to her it was a crime to leave food on your plate. It just was unthinkable to waste food. Because it seemed unnecessary to me as a child to be forced to eat all my food, I tried not to make a big deal about food with my own children. It was there if you wanted it. If you didn't, that was fine too.

I also tried to avoid the inevitable power struggles that often revolve around getting kids to eat enough of their dinner to where you think they might survive one more day. Even half a hot dog is enough, but sometimes a reluctant eater doesn't even want to eat half a dog.

One evening, in desperation, I tried a little reverse psychology on a reluctant eater. I put a piece of hot dog on a fork, held the fork out, and said, "Please don't eat this bite. I love hot dogs, and I really want to eat this bite myself." And then I looked away. And lo and behold, when I looked back, the hot dog was gone. Of course I made a big deal about it. "Oh my gosh! Who ate my bite? Is Captain (the neighborhood dog) under this table? Did Captain eat my bite?" And so I put another bite on the fork, and lo and behold, Captain ate that bite also.

For some reason, this game has worked with every child and every grandchild in our family. I have no idea why. But even vegetables have been consumed by the most reluctant of eaters when the "Who Ate My Bite?" game is played.

| Activity: | Pretending to be astonished when a bite disappears off the fork when the holder of the fork looks away |
|---|---|
| Goal: | Making a game out of getting a few bites into a picky eater |
| Side Benefit: | Realizing you can be more creative than you would have thought |
| Underlying Principle: | If you can make something a game, you can often get the result you are looking for without a power struggle of monumental proportions |

# 41: Six Kids, Six Different Sports

Kendall ran cross-country and track. Christopher played football and threw the discus and shot in track. Adam played baseball and soccer. Amber did track for a while and then switched to horses and trained with a group that square danced on horseback. Courtney played soccer and volleyball. Garrett played basketball and baseball.

So, there you have it. Six kids and six different sports. We were all over the city of Tucson every week, and at tournament time we were all over the state of Arizona. One summer I drove Courtney and several teammates to Phoenix every weekend for elite soccer games.

Why did we do it? Because we genuinely felt that sports had lessons to teach our children that would make a difference in their lives. In order to play sports, they had to be healthy, which meant eating healthy and sleeping healthy. In order to play sports they had to be academically eligible, which meant going to class and getting good grades. And in order to play sports, they had to be manage their time so that the other parts of their lives weren't neglected.

In addition to sports, all three of our sons are Eagle Scouts and all three of our daughters received their Young Womanhood Recognition Award, which is the equivalent of the Eagle Scout award in our church. They had to manage their time. There was no other choice. We helped them the best we could, but we were busy too, and they had to assume responsibility very early for having their uniforms clean, their gear packed and ready, their schedule posted, and so on. We didn't do all of the details for them.

All families are busy, and we were not any busier than any other family. Most of the time, it worked pretty well, and we had a lot of fun participating in and attending the kids' athletic events. I think I can count on one hand the games we missed because of a conflict. We just made it a priority.

| | |
|---|---|
| **Activity:** | Participating in organized activities that teach discipline and keep kids physically healthy |
| **Goal:** | Turning as much responsibility as possible over to them for the logistics of keeping it all running smoothly |
| **Side Benefit:** | Meeting many wonderful people through their participation in athletics, including coaches, other parents, and kids |
| **Underlying Principle:** | Kids need to be busy, and they need to have responsibilities. Sports offer opportunities for both |

# 42: Paul Revere and Other Nonsense

For about twenty years, we had a small cabin on Mt. Lemmon, about an hour from our home. We went up there whenever we could. We really loved it up there in the pine trees, and usually we took our own kids and a car full of their friends.

We had a tradition whenever someone came along for the first time. At bedtime, once the kids were all bedded down in the bunk house, Jim would go out and tell them the story of Paul Revere. The lights would be out, except for a flashlight (do we think he goes anywhere without a flashlight?). He would speak in a low, very soft voice to the very sleepy kids. By the time he got to the part where Paul Revere went door-to-door, knocking and shouting, the kids were pretty much asleep. And so as he would literally run around the room shouting, "the British are coming," the poor child whose first time it was would almost always fall out of bed and onto the floor, so startled that he or she didn't know what to do next. After that, he or she was part of the "in" group in our family.

Jim also had a game he played with the younger children. After dinner, he would look in their ears and tell them what he saw in their stomachs. Of course, he had just watched them eat. However, it nevertheless amazed them that he could actually see the contents of their stomachs.

Often in the car, he took them to River Road where there are hills and curves in the road, and he would tell them to watch and be sure to tell him when a hill or a curve was coming. They would warn him but, of course, he wouldn't hear until he was at the crest of the hill, and then he would yell and shout and convince them he was terrified of the hill ahead and why hadn't they warned him it was coming? They played this game hundreds of times.

You get the idea. There was a lot of nonsense going on much of the time in our family. Jim's great-grandparents had been in Vaudeville and were actors and practical jokers of a rare degree. His grandparents followed suit, and Jim grew up in the midst of pranks and jokes daily. He has a terrific sense of humor and can make the most ordinary thing so silly that you just shake your head in amazement. Obviously, the children loved all this nonsense. They thought he was so funny and so hilarious, and of course he was.

You will notice that none of this cost any money or required any special equipment of any kind, just a creative attitude and a sense of humor.

| | |
|---|---|
| **Activity:** | **Making ordinary things fun** |
| **Goal:** | **Teaching children that even work can be fun and that lightheartedness can always brighten the day** |
| **Side Benefit:** | **Lots of laughter** |
| **Underlying Principle:** | **One of the most important things we can do with our children is teach them how to have fun** |

# 43: Are There Really Clams in Clam Chowder?

Courtney loved clam chowder. She always ordered it when we went out for dinner. And she told everyone about how much she loved it.

One night she was visiting her oldest sister who lived in San Francisco, and they went out for dinner. She ordered clam chowder. Someone at the table mentioned how gritty clams were, and Courtney agreed that clams were really yucky and she would never eat them. At that, her surprised sister replied, "But, Courtney, you *love* clam chowder." After a moment of stunned silence, Courtney breathlessly asked as though she had just discovered a most revolting truth, "You mean there are clams in clam chowder?"

We have all laughed about this story for many years, and it is one of those legends that has lived on and been repeated often whenever someone wants to state the obvious: "Are there clams in clam chowder?"

It also serves to remind us, as parents, that we take a lot for granted in terms of what we think our kids know. We make all kinds of assumptions that they have acquired levels of meaning that not only haven't they acquired but that we assume they can make decisions from.

Things that are routine for us as adults are new and sometimes frightening for children. It never hurts to ask questions: "Do you know what is going to happen here? Do you have any questions before we start this? If you have questions along the way, please ask me. I realize this is new for you and I want to make sure there are no surprises that will scare you."

Driving a car, going to Disneyland for the first time, going to a stage play, opening a bank account, making cookies, visiting someone in a hospital, going to a funeral—taking a few minutes to explain what is about to happen and remind them they can always ask you if something feels unfamiliar and unknown goes a long way to preventing children from being fearful.

| | |
|---|---|
| **Activity:** | **Checking on assumptions** |
| **Goal:** | **Preventing a child from being frightened or embarrassed** |
| **Side Benefit:** | **You as a parent can check on your own assumptions about what you think your child knows and doesn't know** |
| **Underlying Principle:** | **It's always better to ask than to assume you know** |

# 44: Pima County Fair

From the time our first daughter was born, we went to the Pima County Fair every year. I don't think we have ever missed a year. We eat corn dogs, look at all the 4-H projects, walk around the exhibit halls, look at the blue ribbon quilts and jams, and ride the rides. I'm not sure exactly what it is that makes the year seem incomplete without the fair, but it is unthinkable that we would miss it.

Maybe it's that it's so different from every other thing we do. Maybe it's that so many people work so hard to put it all together. Maybe it's that the families of people who assemble and operate the rides are so unique, and their way of life so different from ours. Maybe it's just the smell of the animals, the lure of the Ferris wheel, or the abandonment of all care about healthy food, or some combination of all of these elements, but the fair is a highlight of our year.

We go because we have always gone.

| | |
|---|---|
| **Activity:** | Having yearly treks to the fair |
| **Goal:** | Having an uninterrupted pattern of attendance |
| **Side Benefit:** | The corn dogs |
| **Underlying Principle:** | It's OK to do things that have no purpose other than that you have always done them |

## My Own Notes:

# 45: Animal Lessons

It would be impossible to describe all the lessons our children learned from having animals. At one time or another we had dogs, cats, chickens, goats, sheep, rabbits, horses, desert tortoises, and bees. The first six all had babies, and we all learned about life's cycles through our animals.

Several stories come to mind. One time one of our goats had triplets, all of whom were born deformed. They only lived a few minutes, and it was sad to see these helpless little creatures that had for some reason not formed properly. Another time we had a momma rabbit that ate her own babies. We were all horrified that a mother would do something like that to her young.

The kids frequently brought animals home with them. If there were puppies at the park, we of course had to have one for our menagerie. One time one of the kids brought home a puppy who walked sideways and carried his little head at an angle. We didn't think this puppy could possible live, but it did and it thrived for a long time, even though it continued to walk sideways. Through some logic I can't recall, the kids named him "Smoochers."

We had very mean roosters who would attack the kids as they went into the chicken coop to clean the water buckets. The kids carried garbage can lids as shields to protect themselves.

We had a dog severely injured early one morning when it was attached by a javelina and required sixteen stitches in her backside. We had a springer spaniel who was bit on the nose by a rattlesnake, and his head swelled to twice its normal size. He miraculously survived. We had a neighbor's dog attack our goats and severely injure one to the extent that we had to put her down. That was a very sad day for our family.

We also had many, many wonderful experiences with our animals as we took care of them, cleaned their pens, trimmed their hooves, and gave them names—sometimes silly names (our three sheep were Violet, Vampire, and Vanilla). I milked goats and sold the milk to mothers whose babies were allergic to cow's milk.

Our cats were barn cats who were there to keep the rodents, including snakes, away, and they did so admirably. We also had owls and coyotes that preyed on the cats, and so in a litter of six or seven, we might get one or two to make it a year or more.

I don't know what the kids would say they remember about having animals. But from a parent's perspective, the kids learned how to work and how to be responsible for something other than themselves. Dollar for dollar, having animals was one of our best investments in our children.

| | |
|---|---|
| **Activity:** | **Raising and taking care of animals** |
| **Goal:** | **Teaching children about life** |
| **Side Benefit:** | **Many, many side benefits** |
| **Underlying Principle:** | **As children learn to care for and nurture animals, they seem to realize that all living creatures are worthy of being nurtured** |

# 46: The Mermaid Costume

Our easiest child by far was Amber. She was happy all the time. As an infant, she would play in her crib until someone came and got her. She was just one of those mellow, happy children. If one of the other children took a toy away from her, she would simply get another one. And she would smile while she was doing it. We all marveled at her good nature and wondered where it came from.

When Amber went to first grade, she started acting out in ways that were very troubling to us as her parents. We weren't sure what to do, so I turned to my good friend Stefinee, the wisest of the wise, and Stefinee suggested that Amber didn't know how to be angry. Surely there were situations where she was justified in being angry, but her place in the family was so cemented as the cheerful, happy child that she simply couldn't or wouldn't get angry. I asked Stefinee what we should do.

"Give her to me once a week for a sewing lesson, and I will help her make her Halloween costume. We will go and get the fabric, and then I will watch her sew it and redo it until it's right. That will make her angry. There is nothing worse than ripping out a seam you have just sewn. Then she and I will talk about what it feels like to be angry and how you can express anger in appropriate ways."

So, for the next two months, Amber and Stefinee had a sewing lesson each week. Stefinee made sure that Amber got frustrated and angry. And the behavior at school stopped. And Amber started getting angry at her siblings when they did something ornery to her. And she started sticking up for herself. In short, she learned how to be angry and what to do about it.

And by the way, her mermaid costume was adorable, and she was so very proud that she had made it all by herself!

| | |
|---|---|
| **Activity:** | Sewing |
| **Goal:** | Making a costume for Halloween |
| **Side Benefit:** | Experiencing anger and frustration and learning how to recognize and express it |
| **Underlying Principle:** | Children need to learn how to express anger and be given opportunities for feeling anger and learning how to handle it. Anger is an honest emotion that we all feel, and while there is nothing wrong with feeling anger, where we get in trouble is when we don't know how to express it and work through it |

# Addendum

## INTRODUCTION

Because of my academic background, I am continually drawn to the theories of learning that seem to have so much application to parenting. I thought about introducing this book with these theories, but wanted the stories to stand alone, without the organizing underpinnings of the theories at the outset. However, now that you have read the stories and vignettes about the life of our family, perhaps the theories will add a different dimension. For those of you who might actually want to study your parenting and take a more systematic approach, these theories may give you a foundation for a thoughtful examination of your own parenting.

See what you think as you read through what I think is very interesting and very applicable information. I hope you will agree.

There are dozens and dozens of developmental theories that have application to parenting. It is beyond the scope of this book to delve deeply into any of them, and I only introduce four here that each seem to capture a very different element of the parenting endeavor.

Baumrind's parenting styles or management styles have such wide application in the workplace as well as in the family that they are a useful framework to have at your fingertips.

Vygotsky's zone of proximal development describes the continual interaction in parenting between a more knowledgeable learner and a less knowledgeable learner in such an elegant way that you will see these zones in virtually all you do with your children.

Maslow's hierarchy of needs reminds us that unless needs that are lower on the hierarchy are met, it is difficult if not impossible to move up to higher-level engagement.

And Piaget's theory has been so foundational in the field of developmental psychology because it captures the changing nature of theory building that goes on in the child's mind continually.

## BAUMRIND'S PARENTING STYLES

> **Advance Organizer:** "I was raised in a military family. I answered my dad with 'Yes, sir' and 'No, sir.' When he said something, we obeyed, even if we didn't agree. There was never any room for discussion. Rules were rules, and they were meant to be obeyed. He used words such as 'insubordinate' if we questioned something or weren't quick enough to do what he asked. Not that he was a mean person; he wasn't. He was just a military man. I want to do things differently when I have children, but I have no clue how to organize my thinking about what makes a good parent. I want to allow my kids to have opinions and show them a little more respect. I want us to reach conclusions together about certain things. But I realize there's comfort in having someone else make all the decisions. It sort of relieves you of any responsibility. So, as I think about how I might want to be different, I get scared."

Diana Baumrind was the first to categorize differing styles in parenting. These categories are extremely helpful in thinking about ourselves and how we react in different situations in the parenting enterprise. Baumrind's parenting styles help us see ourselves within a framework that makes sense and we can all apply. It is important to keep these three caveats in mind:
1. Although we each respond predominantly in one style, we do move back and forth among all the styles.
2. In a family, there may be several styles operating. Mom may have one style, Dad another, Grandma a third, and your caregiver a fourth.

3. Different children react to these styles differently. In other words, children aren't empty vessels; they come to us with personalities and preferences that impact the way we parent.

Baumrind began her work with three styles that were eventually expanded to four. The four styles, in a nutshell, are as follows. You will probably immediately see yourself in one of these styles and say, "That's me!"
- The **authoritarian style** parent is obedience oriented. Orders are expected to be obeyed without explanation. Authoritarian parents provide very structured environments with clearly stated rules. Two types of authoritarian parents are:
    - Nonauthoritarian-directive parents, who are directive but not intrusive. In other words these parents give direction but not in a commanding way.
    - Authoritarian-directive, who are highly intrusive. These parents are very demanding of immediate obedience with no questions asked.
- The **authoritative style** parent is both demanding and responsive. Clear standards are set; parents are assertive but not intrusive and restrictive. Disciplinary methods are supportive rather than punitive. Goals are to teach children to be assertive, socially responsible, self-regulated, and cooperative.
- The **indulgent style** parent is often referred to as permissive. The indulgent parent is not demanding but rather lenient, allows considerable self-regulation on the part of the child, avoids confrontation, and does not require mature behavior. An indulgent parent can be:
    - Democratic and engaged with the child, or
    - Nondirective and fairly unengaged
- The **uninvolved style** parent is neither responsive to his or her children nor demanding. In extreme cases, this style becomes neglectful and rejecting, although it is possible to be uninvolved and still fall within the normal range of parenting.

Let's go back to the three caveats for a minute. The first states that we move back and forth among the styles. Circumstances sometimes provide opportunities or even demand a certain style. For example, perhaps my child is sick and resting on the couch with all the required blankets, pillows, and stuffed animals, feeling lousy. I may have some rules about what my child can eat at certain times during the day. Perhaps I want him to have a nutritious breakfast before going off to school. However, today, I may give him ginger ale and ice cream for breakfast. I am behaving like an indulgent parent because the situation allows it.

On the other hand, if my three-year-old is about to run out into the street to retrieve a soccer ball, and I see an oncoming car, I am not likely to say, "Oh, honey, I wish you would reconsider that decision. Can we talk about it?" I am more likely to grab the child by the arm if I am near enough or yell loudly something like "Don't you dare go out in that street. There's a car coming. Stop right now!" I am behaving like an authoritarian parent because the situation demands it.

Most people identify themselves as authoritative parents, which is not surprising given our democratic culture. Although most of us identify with one style or another, in certain situations we may appropriately adopt a different style because the circumstances either allow or demand it. This is exactly as it should be, and we shouldn't feel guilty for becoming authoritarian or permissive when we feel it's needed.

The second caveat is a little trickier. What happens in a family when Mom is authoritarian and Dad is indulgent? Or what happens when a child's caregiver is authoritarian and Mom is indulgent? Interestingly, kids are both perceptive and resilient in understanding that the framework in one setting is different than the framework in another. So, a daycare versus home difference will be understood by most children. But when two very different styles are being enacted in the same home, that can produce confusion for a child, and an opportunity to manipulate the situation for older children who quickly figure out how to do this. Mom (the authoritarian parent) says "no, absolutely not," to something, so the child goes to Dad (the indulgent parent) and gets a "sure, that sounds like fun" response. You can be thinking about how you communicate in your family when styles differ.

The third caveat is that, as parents, we respond to different children differently. We can afford to be more indulgent with an "easy" child who wants to please, is complaint, and does what we ask. It's also easy to be authoritarian with a "difficult" child who questions everything, rarely does what we ask (at least the first time), and seems to delight in antagonizing his or her siblings.

In short, the parenting milieu is very interactive. We are responding to a highly charged environment where the following ingredients are all present: our perceptions of ourselves, our self-esteem, our own histories as children, our knowledge, our age, our health, our finances, our work and living circumstances, the number of children in our family, the makeup of biological children/adopted children/blended children/foster children, the characteristics of the children themselves, how they relate to one another, how they relate to us, and extended family members present on occasion or all the time, just to name a few.

This is a highly complex, often chaotic, always emotionally charged environment, and we function in it 24/7. It is the hub of our lives around which we build the other things: work, play, friends, and recreation. Understanding our parenting styles can help us all understand the decisions we make as parents a little better, and to give information that will aid in making future decisions. It is said that an elementary teacher makes a thousand decisions a day by answering questions and and responding to requests such as "can I go to the bathroom, can I get a drink, I lost my pencil, my head hurts, where's my book, Sam is bothering me, etc." Parents easily make that many decisions a day or more. Becoming the best decision makers can help us maximize our ability to influence our children in positive directions, which is what we all want.

**Questions for you to consider:**

- What parenting styles were evident in the home where you grew up?
- What style do you employ in your own home?
- What other styles do your children come in contact with in school, daycare, and other homes?

**Vygotsky's Zone of Proximal Development**

> **Advance Organizer:** "I remember the first time I used Quicken, the software for organizing your finances. I loaded the software onto my computer and started to plow through it myself. I was quickly lost and very frustrated. After a couple of hours I just put it all away. A week later, I was at my friend's house and mentioned to her my disastrous first attempt to use Quicken. She said she had used it for years and would show me how if I wanted her to. We sat down at her computer and in an hour, I felt like I could do all the things I wanted to do. Why was it so much easier when she just showed me the same things I had been trying to figure out myself?"

Lev Vygotsky was a Russian psychologist who captured elements of the learning environment in ways that no one had before him. He suggested that most learning takes place in a social environment between people. That is certainly true in a family. Children are learning from parents, and at the same time they are learning from siblings, friends, teachers, coaches, tutors, neighbors, and a whole host of other people. And parents are learning from children.

Vygotsky suggested that much of what we learn is accomplished between a person with less knowledge or expertise and a person with more knowledge or expertise. Think about a piano teacher, for example. A beginning piano student has no idea was a scale is, or a sharp or a flat. But after several months of working with a good piano teacher, the keyboard now looks familiar, and several songs have been mastered. Vygotsky suggested that the difference between what that beginning piano student could do by him- or herself as a novice and what he or she could do under the tutelage of an expert is the zone of proximal development.

Basically this is the difference between what I can do on my own and what I can do with help. It is within this zone that much learning occurs. An older sister helps a younger sister learn to tie her shoes; an older brother helps a younger brother do his homework; a coach helps a beginning baseball player learn to slide into first base; a Girl Scout leader helps her troop manage their cookie sales and learn many organizing skills in the process. These are all examples of the zone of proximal development.

This is a very powerful way to look at learning within a family. There are many zones operating in parallel, some overt and some hidden. Many of us have had the experience of watching children do something we had no idea they knew how to do, only to find out that they had learned how by repeatedly watching someone in the family do it. Some of us have been embarrassed by the things our children learned to say and do when we didn't know they were watching and listening to us!

A zone of development is a compelling framework in a family for several reasons. First, responsibility shifts from the more experienced learner to the less experienced learner throughout the zone. Once the piano student has mastered the scales, then the teacher places the responsibility on the student for knowing them in the future. That responsibility no longer rests with the teacher. Once the baseball player knows how to slide, the coach expects her to do it correctly from then on. The responsibility is on her shoulders and not the coach's any longer.

Isn't this what parenting children is all about—helping those for whom we have responsibility for a few short years become proficient decision makers themselves? It starts with what to have for breakfast—Rice Krispies or Cheerios—and moves to bigger and more complicated decisions as they grow. But the end result, we hope, is young adults who have had ample opportunity to make decisions, see and understand the consequences, learn from those consequences, and get better at the process.

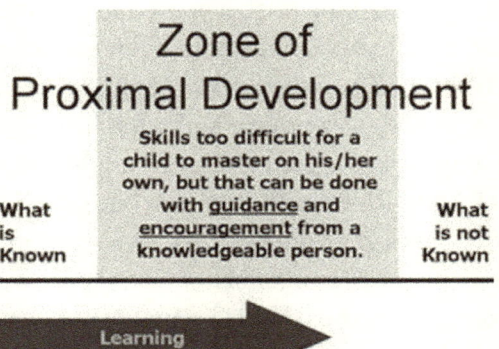

Second, we live in a social world. We learn in classrooms, we work in teams at work, we play on teams in sports, and we relax with friends. So, understanding ourselves the dynamics of learning from others helps us to be better learners as parents, and that translates into the ability to provide more effective learning environments for the children whom we parent.

**Questions for you to consider:**

- What were some of the important zones of proximal development in your early years?
- What about them was memorable to you?
- How do you create zones for others in your life today?
- What do you think the elements of an effective zone are?

Let us say here, for the record, that families come in all shapes and sizes. A single person is a family unit as much as an extended family with parents, children, and grandchildren all living in one home. Both heterosexual and gay couples make up families, and many parent children. Many grandparents are raising their grandchildren today. Young people who have been adjudicated by the court live on their own or with other older teens and function as a family unit. The definition of a family today is broad and varied, and this book is intended to be of use to all kinds of families in all kinds of circumstances.

This book has application for a variety of professionals, including volunteers, who work with children and young people—teachers, nurses, afterschool program coordinators, summer program coordinators, coaches, and people who offer parenting classes, to name a few. Children often find role models in unlikely places, and you never know when a child is looking to you to provide him or her with a model for how an adult thinks, acts, and interacts with the world.

## MASLOW'S HIERARCHY OF NEEDS

Sometimes it's helpful to be able to put things into categories. One of the reasons that stage theories are so appealing is that we can look at the stages and see where we fit and why. Maslow's hierarchy of needs is a stage theory that almost everyone knows. Maslow proposed an ascending hierarchy of needs in the order that they must be met before a person can move onto the next higher level, as the figure below illustrates.

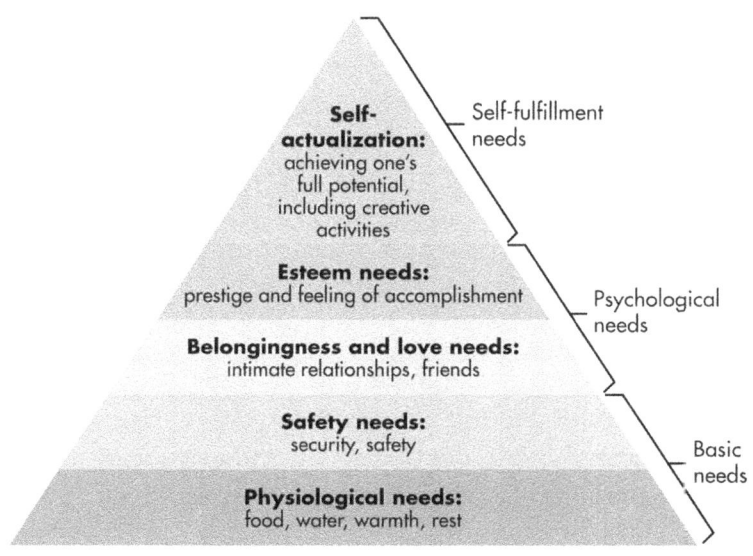

One moves up the hierarchy as each set of needs is met, ultimately reaching the highest stage of self-actualization. It is fairly easy to look at the stages and see where we, or others we know, are located.

---

**Questions for you to consider:**

- How does Maslow's hierarchy affect the way you interact with children when they are tired, unhappy, cold, hungry, or otherwise out of sorts?
- How can Maslow's hierarchy help you understand your child's needs at the moment?

---

## PIAGET'S STAGE THEORY OF DEVELOPMENT

**Advance Organizer:** "My four year old said the cutest thing yesterday. He said his truck is alive. When I asked him why, he said 'Because it moves.' So, I decided to ask my eight year old 'What is alive?' She said, 'Things are alive if they breathe and grow. Plants grow, so they're alive. People breathe and grow so they're alive.' I thought that was a pretty good answer. Then I started to wonder, what happens between the age of four and the age of eight that changes a child's understanding of something so basic as what is alive?"

In a similar fashion, the Swiss psychologist Jean Piaget proposed a theory of cognitive development with four discrete stages. Children think differently in each of the stages based on the cognitive skills they have acquired, which Piaget called cognitive structures. For the purposes of parenting, it does little good to insist a child execute a behavior for which he or she does not have the prerequisite cognitive structure.

For example, to ask a two-year-old to understand that she has hurt someone's feelings is an exercise in futility because the ability to take the perspective of another person isn't acquired until the preoperational stage between the ages of two and seven. It is also futile to insist that a five-year-old boy wear his sister's pink jacket, over his strenuous objections because it's a "girlie coat." Not until age seven will he begin to "conserve," as Piaget called it, and understand that changes in appearance do not change the essence of an object or a person. At age five, he fears that wearing a girl's coat will change him into a girl!

The table below gives an overview of Piaget's stages and the cognitive abilities that are acquired in each stage. It seems reasonable that if a child can't understand the logic underlying a particular request, it is unlikely that he or she will be able to accomplish that request for very long. On the contrary, if the logic is apparent, we have a much greater chance for success.

## STAGES OF COGNITIVE DEVELOPMENT

| Stage | Characterized by | Implications for Parents |
|---|---|---|
| **Sensori-motor** (Birth to two years) | Differentiates self from objects<br><br>Recognizes self as agent of action and begins to act intentionally: for example, pulls a string to set a mobile in motion or shakes a rattle to make a noise<br><br>Achieves object permanence: realizes that things continue to exist even when they are no longer present to the senses | The "terrible twos" is an outcome of a child realizing that he or she is a separate person with a will that can be exercised, often loudly!<br><br>Manipulating objects to see what happens is a great game that infants love to play—how many times can a nine-month-old drop food on the floor just to make sure the law of gravity still works!<br><br>When object permanence is achieved, a child realizes that Mommy is in the next room and not gone forever, that feet do not disappear in shoes, and that going to sleep is not the end of life! |
| **Preoperational** (two to seven years) | Learns to use language and to represent objects by images and words<br><br>Thinking is still egocentric: has difficulty taking the viewpoint of others<br><br>Classifies objects by a single feature: for example, groups together all the red blocks regardless of shape or all the square blocks regardless of color | Language is the great accomplishment of these five years—the ability to use and understand a complicated system of verbal expression.<br><br>It is difficult if not impossible for a preoperational child to empathize with the feelings of others.<br><br>The ability to categorize helps to make sense of a complicated world. Single-feature classification means that all veggies are yucky, all medicine tastes bad, anyone wearing a hat is scary, all dogs bite, and all forms of water are wonderful! |

| | | |
|---|---|---|
| **Concrete operational** (seven to eleven years) | Can think logically about objects and events<br><br>Achieves conservation of number (age six), mass (age seven), and weight (age nine)<br><br>Classifies objects according to several features and can order them in series along a single dimension such as size | The hallmark of logical thinking occurs in this stage. Children of seven can wait for their desires to be fulfilled, can understand the logic in reward and time out, and can understand cause and effect.<br><br>The skill of conservation allows children to understand that surface changes do not alter the essence of an object, so wearing his sister's pink sweater does not change a boy's maleness, for example.<br><br>Children can now hold more than one dimension in mind at the same time, so they can understand that although yesterday you said you were taking them to the movie, that is not possible now because something changed. |
| **Formal operational** (eleven years and up) | Can think logically about abstract propositions and test hypotheses systematically<br><br>Becomes concerned with the hypothetical, the future, and ideological problems | Things get fun in this stage. You can propose hypothetical situations to children such as what do you think will happen if you continue to not do your homework, or pick on your sibling?<br><br>Hypothetical constructs such as enough food for all, world peace, and even family peace become possible ideas to think about. |

Piaget's contributions to the field of child development were vast. The innovative tasks that he devised to unlock a child's thinking are still in use today in the field of developmental psychology. Some of the important takeaways from Piaget include the following:

- A child's ability to understand the world around him or her and to reason accurately about that world changes over time in predictable ways.

- A child's ability to comply with a parent or teacher's request may depend on whether he or she has acquired the underlying logic of that request.
- Children differ in how and when they acquire these skills, although there are general patterns that seem to apply to most children

Piaget proposed that the essence of child development is the acquisition of something he called "cognitive structures." We acquire thousands of these cognitive structures as we grow to adulthood, and it is through these structures that we interpret the world around us. For example, a young child thinks an airplane is alive because it flies. In a way, that makes perfect sense. Birds fly, and they are alive; bees fly, and they are alive; so why shouldn't an airplane be alive? Over time, as a child acquires an understanding of biology, he or she refines the cognitive structure for "what is alive" further and further until a comprehensive system of organizing things that are alive emerges. This takes many years and many experiences. And so it is with most cognitive structures.

Piaget's theory is applicable to the content of this book in a variety of ways. First, if we can understand how a child is thinking at a given time in his or her life, we can better fit our parenting strategies to match what the child is capable of understanding. Second, we can assist the child in moving forward through the stages by explaining the way we think about things and thus exposing the child to our own cognitive structures. Think of the difference in the following bedtime scenarios:

1. Your bedtime is 8:00 p.m. for many reasons. First, it's important for you to get enough sleep so you can grow, your body can repair itself, and you can feel rested. Second, I need some "down time" in the evening to do things that I can't do when you are up. And third, your body needs to know that it will be able to go to sleep

at the same time every night. That helps your body "learn" to go to sleep.
2. I really don't care when you go to bed; that's up to you. When you are tired, just go put yourself to bed.
3. You will go to bed at 8:00 p.m. because I said so.

---

**Questions for you to consider:**

- At what age would the first scenario be effective?
- What scenarios could be effective at earlier ages?
- What would be the benefits of having this conversation with a child?
- Would you need to do this every time?

---

I have barely scratched the surface here of developmental theories that have application to parenting, even the four so briefly discussed here. There are many very good developmental theory books, if you have an interest in learning more about theory bases of how we grow and learn from a developmental perspective.

Life is many things. Among the richest treasures life has to offer are the experiences from which we learn who we are, how we understand the world, and how we can be the best we are capable of being. That is our desire for ourselves, and it is certainly our desire for our children.

As I write this book, I have recently turned sixty-eight years old. My grandmother was elderly at sixty-eight. My mother seemed much younger at sixty-eight than my grandmother did. And I, at sixty-eight, feel much younger than my mother did. So, developmental trajectories change over the decades. Nutrition, education, health, and experience all play a role in our developmental path. I expect to live into my nineties and be productive until I pass away. That is my plan and my intention. In many ways, I have more energy now than I did when I was younger and raising a family.

The important thing is for us to realize that we have an influence on those around us—especially children. Neighbor children, children we see at church, and the children of our friends all are influenced by the ways we interact with them. No matter what our age or what our circumstances, we can take the information from this book and other sources and impact children's learning experiences. We can help them see the wonder of learning and the wonder of the world around them. It is my hope that we will all engage ourselves and the children with whom we associate in this quest.

www.ingramcontent.com/pod-product-compliance
Lightning Source LLC
Chambersburg PA
CBHW020853090426
42736CB00008B/355